Copyright

Digital ISBN 978-0-9893135-2-0
Paperback/Hardcover ISBN 978-0-9893135-3-7

Follow our journey:

@ChrisRSiegfried
@DesHartsock

Designed, Created and Published by @ZackKalter.

Dedication

To my loving family, thank you for your support throughout the years.
I wouldn't be who I am without you!

To my beautiful fiancee Desiree, thank you for encouraging me to publish my poetry and open my heart to the world.

I love you.

Contents

Cover Explanation

The cover of this book was carefully planned and laid out with different meaning behind various elements on the page. While I wanted to keep the cover simplistic in nature, I want to take a minute and share with you what the cover represents. As you may or may not know, this poetic journey of mine started in 2009 and has helped me navigate my emotions through the ups and downs of professional baseball - and most recently through my journey to find the love of my life, Desiree Hartsock.

The tear in the baseball represents me opening up my heart and soul and pouring everything I have into baseball and my relationship with Des. The stitches on the heart symbolize all the good and the bad that comes along with both baseball and relationships - they keep everything held together. The two bumps at the top of the heart signify two people coming together, which is why I chose to have the silhouette of me and Des in the middle.

The title "Diamonds + Hearts: A Poetic Memoir" is a metaphor for the baseball diamonds I played on everyday of my life where I worked so hard to do the best I could to be the best player. I chose the word "hearts" because it gives the readers a look into the love story that unfolds within the memoirs and the journey of my love life with Des. Is it ironic that the initials of Diamonds and Hearts are also the initials of the woman I will be spending the rest of my life with? I hope you enjoy these poems.

Foreword

A lot of time has passed between my first and most recent piece of writing. With each day, new, exciting, encouraging and sometimes challenging obstacles were placed in front of me. The most important thing I learned throughout this poetic journey was that no matter how I was feeling, writing it down felt like lifting a load of over 1000 pounds off of my shoulders. Do I consider myself a poet? No. Do the pieces I write necessarily make sense or read in perfect iambic pentameter? Maybe not. Writing poetry was nothing more than an outlet for me to express my feelings and capture those feelings in writing - a journal of my life if you will. While this journey was just a small piece of my life, it partially defines who I am today.

While reading this poetic biography, enjoy it for what it is - an emotional journey through words. Read into it. Ponder. Try to think about the words as a story of my daily activities or the roles people were playing in my life. Read into the monotony of some and share in the passionate love stories of others. If you feel they relate to you in any shape or form, let me know. I have provided a brief synopsis of each piece so that you can have a better understanding of where my mind, heart and body were at during the time of writing.

You may ask yourself why I am sharing this piece of my life with you. To be honest, the answer is this: so many of us have stories to tell or experiences to share but never get the opportunity to share them with others. People always ask me if I am tired of telling others how my baseball career went or how my experience on a dating reality show was. I never get tired of sharing these stories with others because it makes me happy knowing others can experience a piece of what I've experienced through my stories and poetry. Not everyone gets to play professional baseball or go on a reality TV show looking to find love and I feel it is my duty to share these once in a lifetime experiences with those who may not get these unique opportunities.

I am thankful for these opportunities. I am thankful for my friends. I am thankful for my family and the support they give me everyday and in days passed. I hope you can enjoy this poetic biography and understand that I am thankful for having the opportunity to share it with you. I am truly blessed. Thank you for picking up this book and enjoy it to the fullest!

With Warmest Regards,

Chris Siegfried

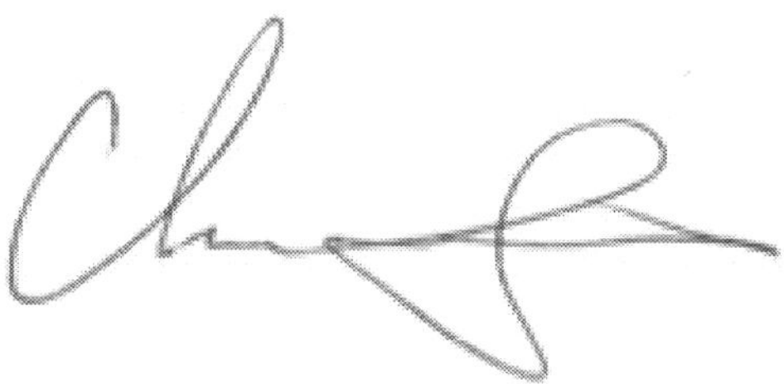

Diamonds

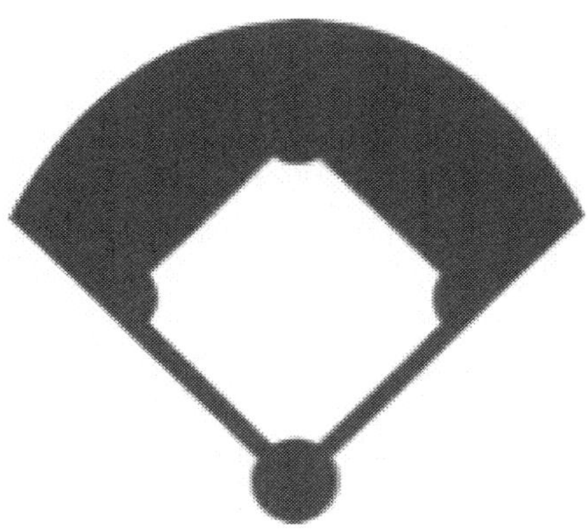

1. Observations

Date: April 21, 2009
Time: 5:45 PM
Location: Mesa, Arizona

"Observations"

To sit and listen can be quite calming,
Although the noises sometimes alarming.

You look around and see different faces,
Their minds run rampant, each has their twitches.

While some read papers,
Others chat on their phones.
Some just sit,
Watching everyone, people watching.

The observer,
He who is still writing,

Has many observations,
Within these walls confining.

As the pencil lay down,
His head on a swivel,
He enjoys the company,
Of the randomness of people.

Synopsis

I wrote this poem on a whim while I as sitting enjoying an americano coffee at Starbucks one day after work. Enjoy the randomness of the poetry here and imagine yourself sitting and people watching!

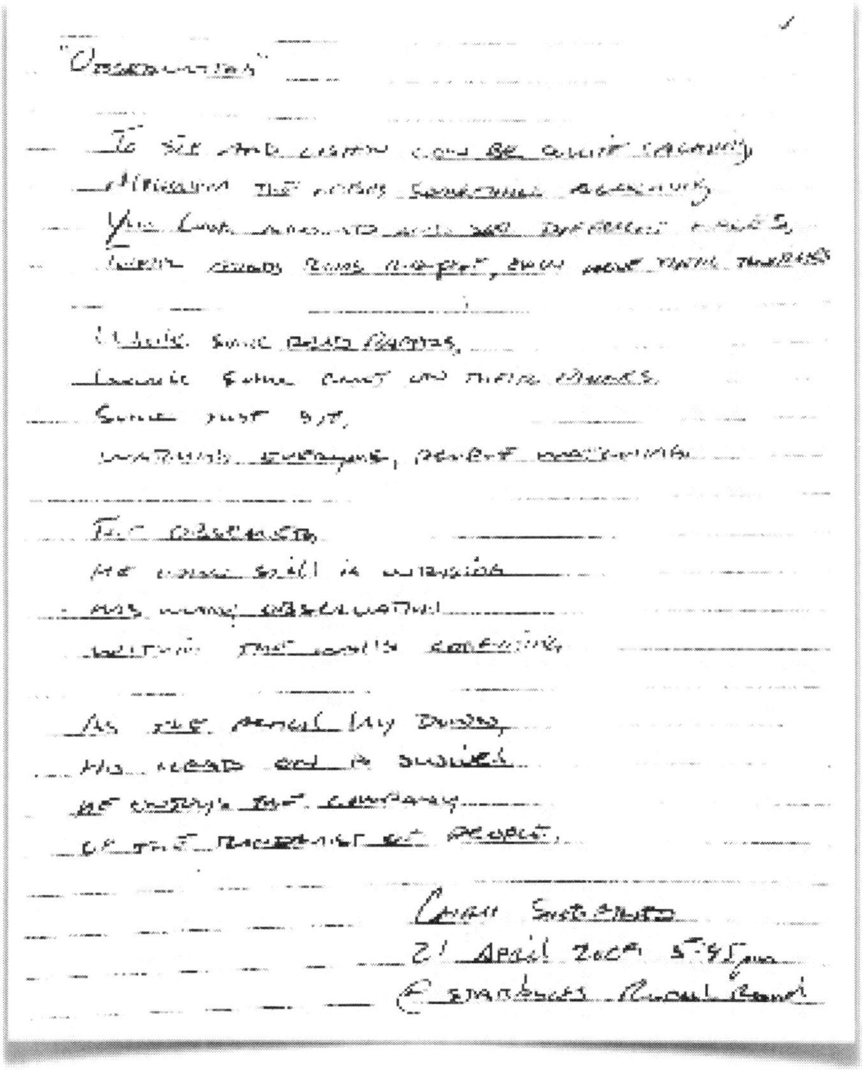
"Observation"

To see and listen can be quite calming

[illegible] the [illegible] something [illegible]

You can [illegible] different faces,

[illegible]

While some read papers,

[illegible] on their phones.

Some just sit,

watching everyone, [illegible]

The observer

[illegible]

[illegible] observation

[illegible]

As the pencil lay down,

His head [illegible] a smile.

He enjoy'd the company

of the [illegible] of people.

[illegible]

21 April 200[illegible] 5:45pm

@ Starbucks [illegible]

2. Thoughts

Date: April 21 2009
Time: 5:05 PM
Location: Mesa, Arizona

"Thoughts"

As I sit in this leather bound chair,
The smell of coffee in the air.

The golden rays of summer bare,
A warm sensation one may not dare…**AVOID**.

I think of all the things I've done,
All the thoughts that run among,

The electric impulses in my head,
The thoughts don't stop as I lay to bed…**DAILY**.

When I recall the feelings of,
All the ones I used to love.

The sensations greatly full of joy,
Yet years do pass and I do not deploy…**DOUBT**.

Doubt for which the choices made,
Bad or good the feelings stray.
Though all come adrift when I am alone,
They make me stronger each day of old.

Synopsis

I really do enjoy country music and the song that inspired me to write this piece was a song written by David Allen Coe. While some may not agree with his lyrics, sometimes you just have to sit back and enjoy the tune. This might be the most, if not one of the most, unique poems I've ever written. When I was writing this piece I let my mind wonder and just put the pen to paper. Again I was sitting in a Starbucks, something I took a liking to during my stay in Arizona. The interesting characteristic to you that may stand out is the ending of every stanza.

Avoid, Daily, Doubt.

Interesting back story here: during my stay in extended spring training I did have thoughts about what I should be doing…baseball, finish school, start a career, etc. The one thing that kept me focused outside of some of the books I read was the continued support I received from family and friends and the hunger to achieve what it was I was after - making it to the big leagues! The words avoid daily doubt randomly came to me at the end of each stanza and it wasn't until after that I realized there was a hidden message in my own work. My own work was speaking to me and it took me by surprise!

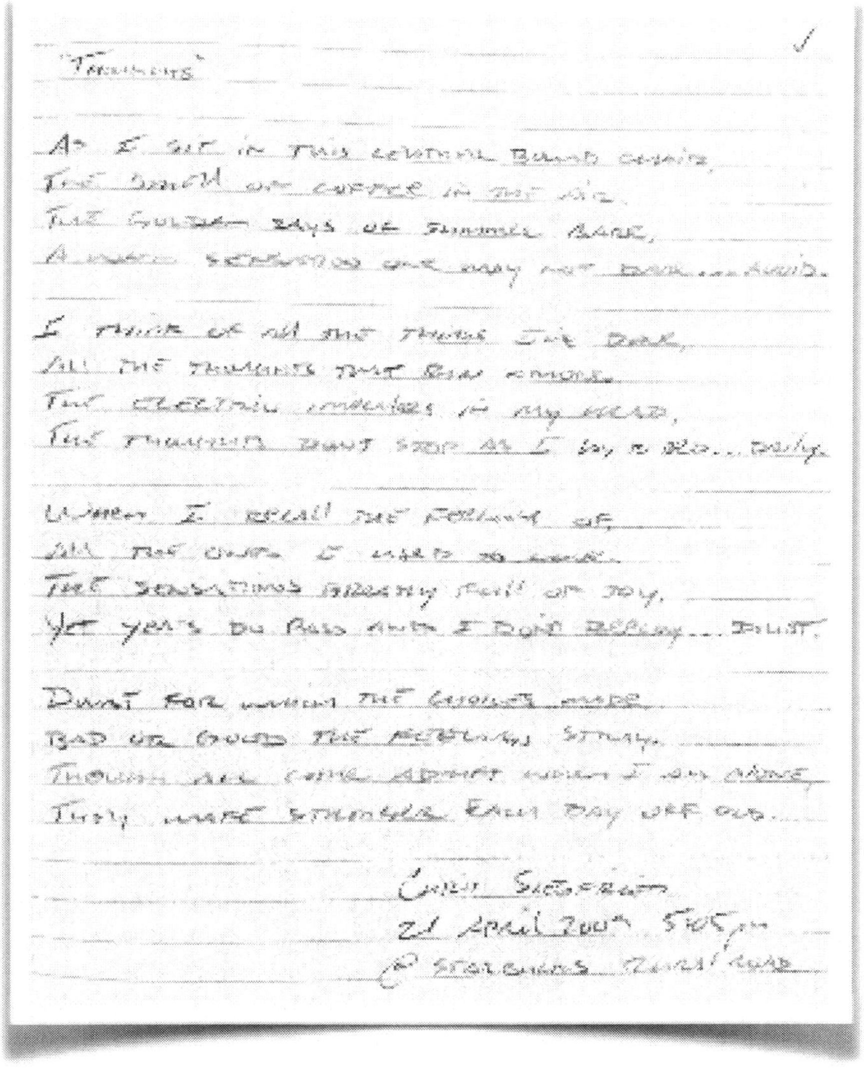

"Thoughts"

As I sit in this leather bound chair,
The smell of coffee in the air,
The golden days of summer [illegible],
A [illegible] sensation one may not [illegible]...

I think of all the things I've done,
All the thoughts that [illegible],
The electric images in my head,
The thoughts don't stop as I lay to bed... daily.

When I recall the feelings of
All the ones I used to know,
The sensations [illegible] full of joy,
Yet years do pass and I don't [illegible]... [illegible].

What for [illegible] the choices made
Bad or good the feelings stay.
Though all come about when I am alone,
They make stronger each day we're old...

Chris Siegfried
21 April 2004 5:05pm
@ Starbucks [illegible] Road

3. Labor Not-So-Intensive

Date: April 22, 2009
Time: 3:45pm
Location: Mesa, Arizona

"Labor Not-So-Intensive"

As I labor through the day,
I think of things that brought me this way.

The insecurities people have,
Make me ever so strong and not quite mad.

Even with the constant banter,
I push through the day and listen to what really matters.

With every opinion an ear shot away,
How does one choose which to obey?

I use what got me to this point,
The drive, the sweat, hope and the tears.

That one day soon all of this work,
Will pay for itself, family front row and near.

Until I find myself amongst,
The day I work so hard to see,

I will enjoy all the hard times,
And do what I know is best for me.

Synopsis

During this point in my baseball career I was tired of hearing fellow teammates complain about their situation and where they were within the organization. The title of this poem is meant to give the reader the idea that while some ball players feel that baseball is hard and repetitive and would rather be playing video games in their hotel room, others do not take for granted the opportunity and train hard every minute of their day. It is laborious yes, but it is a game that we were given the ability to play. The "work," if you want to call it that, is not that hard. Rather, the work of taking ground balls and throwing bullpens and hitting batting practice is fun and not really work at all!

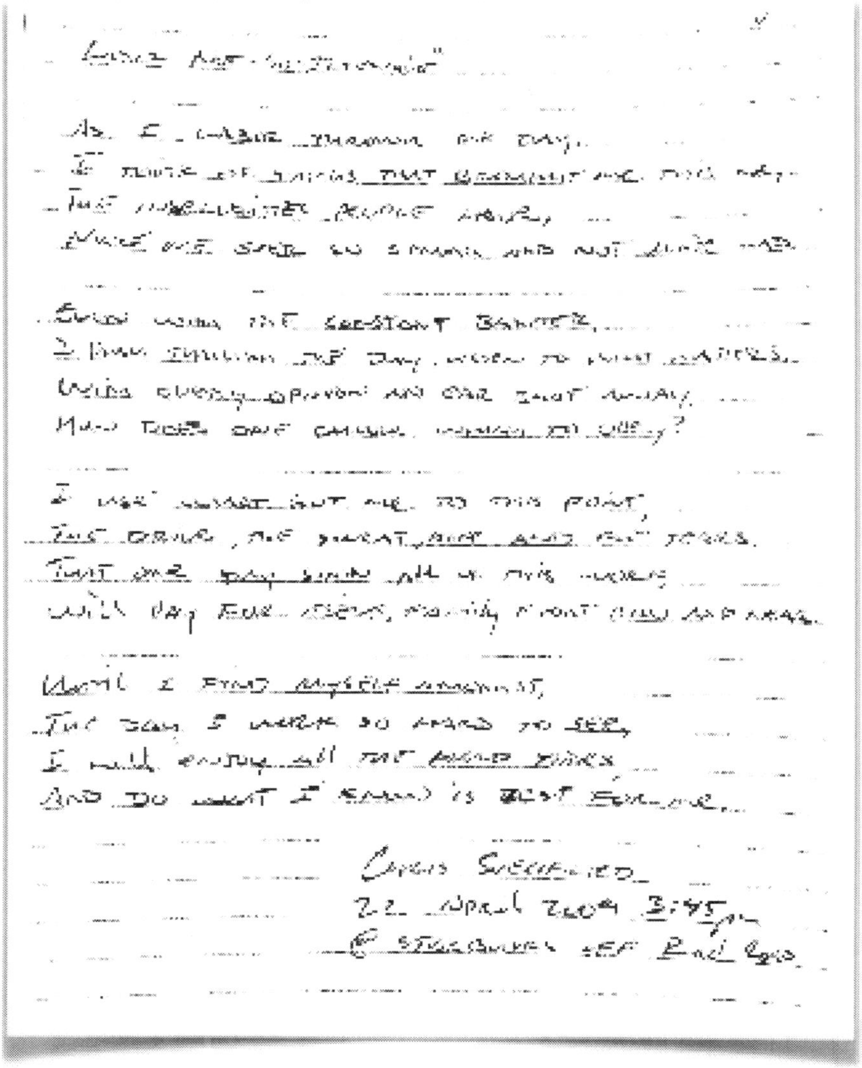

As I walk through the day,

Until I find myself again,

22 April 2009 3:45pm

4. Standing Out They're

Date: April 28, 2009
Time: 5:45pm
Location: Mesa, Arizona

"Standing Out They're"

Every day we talk about the same things.
Are they truly happy inside?

There is no room for the mind to grow.
The conversation empty of thought.

Words just run, like a mudslide down a bank.
Never thinking about the task at hand.

The topics of conversation somewhat vary:
Girls, food, money, drinking, insomnia.

Everyone lives in the past.
"Man when I was in college…"

No one wants to be in the now, right here.
But all chose to do this as a profession.

Is it a job or a game or both?
Some don't want to work and hate to play, everyday.

Fighting is as regular as the sun is shining.

People always talk behind each other's back.

For at least one hour a day, everything is wrong.
My legs, my arm, my back; they are all hurting.

Everything seems to take forever.
Tomorrow we will have to do it all again.

Synopsis

Now I have to admit that being in the outfield chasing down fly balls for the hitters during batting practice was not the best time of the season. It happened EVERY day. As we stood out there roasting under the hot, summer, Midwest sun all people could talk about was the night before and tell stories of years passed when we all lived in our glory days of college.

Don't get me wrong, I sometimes joined in on those conversations, but what I found the most interesting was how people complained so much about being at the level they were at or not getting more opportunities and how they were being treated poorly. We all had the opportunity that comes once in a lifetime and there was no reason to do everything one could to make the most of it. Some did, while others did not. We got to play the game of baseball and get paid for it! How cool is that?

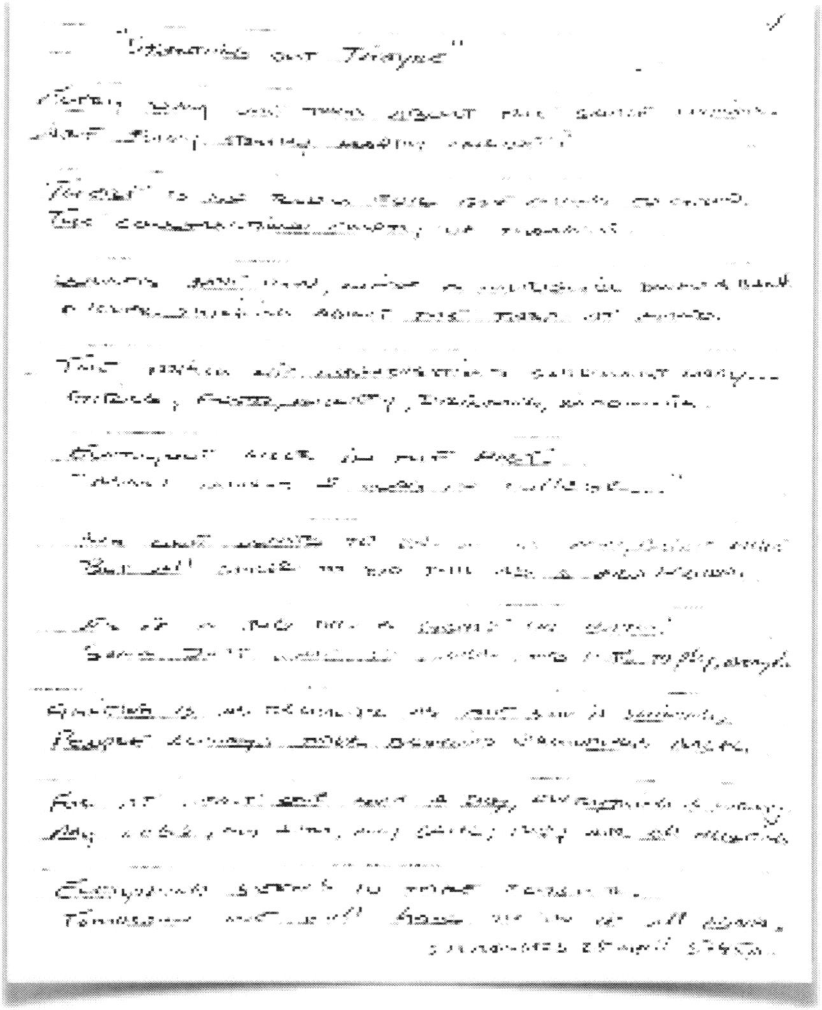

5. Extended Repetition

Date: April 29, 2009
Time: 5:35 PM
Location: Mesa, Arizona

"Extended Repetition"

The morning will start before the sun will rise.
I get up and drink water to start the day.

My roommate still asleep or at least pretends.
Shower first for it is my turn; he'll sleep ten more minutes.

We exchange our greetings, both still half awake.
I get ready and sit and think about the day.

We head to breakfast, one hundred yards away.
We always drive because we take off right after.

Not much is said on the way to the field.
There are now five guys in the car, all weary.

It's now just after six o'clock in the locker room.
I sit down and plan my day, afterwards I say hi to the guys.

The time has come to run outside, but first we stretch.

The running is never hard, yet all complain.

I head inside to do my workout, it's 7:15a.
My early work is done by 8:00a.

We meet with the coaches and head to stretch, AGAIN.
The stretching program is half-hearted.

Fundamentals start around 8:30am.
Throwing is usually cut short due to time constraints…
what do we do again?

The time is now 9:30a and all pitchers must shag.
Instead of getting work done, we stand around for an hour.

It's now 10:30a and we all run inside to relax.
The game starts in thirty minutes.

I prepare myself to pitch.
I always know when I am pitching, not realistic.

As I finish my performance, I watch some film.
My coaches critique me for about five minutes…thanks.

I head inside to run, lift and do my shoulder work…
AGAIN.
Afterwards, I will ice my arm if I feel it is necessary.
The locker room is my next stop.
There I will shower and take my vitamins.

The time is now 2:00p.
My baseball day has finished and I head home.

Tomorrow will be the same…

Synopsis

Here I wanted to give the reader a little insight into the day of the average baseball player's life during extended spring training. During this time, I was working on a few mechanical pitching creases in my delivery that needed to be "ironed" out if you will. The best way to go about your days in extended spring training is to always focus on your goal and your purpose in professional baseball - the dream of making it to the big leagues! You have to be careful to not get sucked into the monotony of the everyday grind.

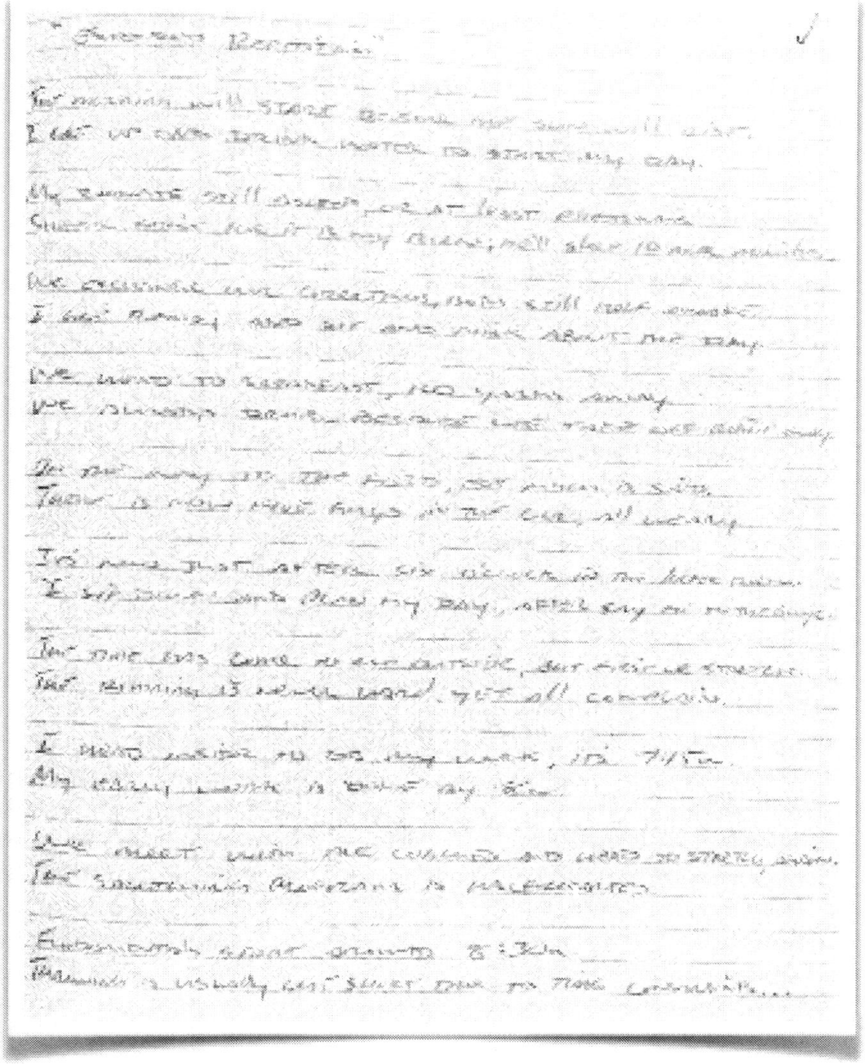

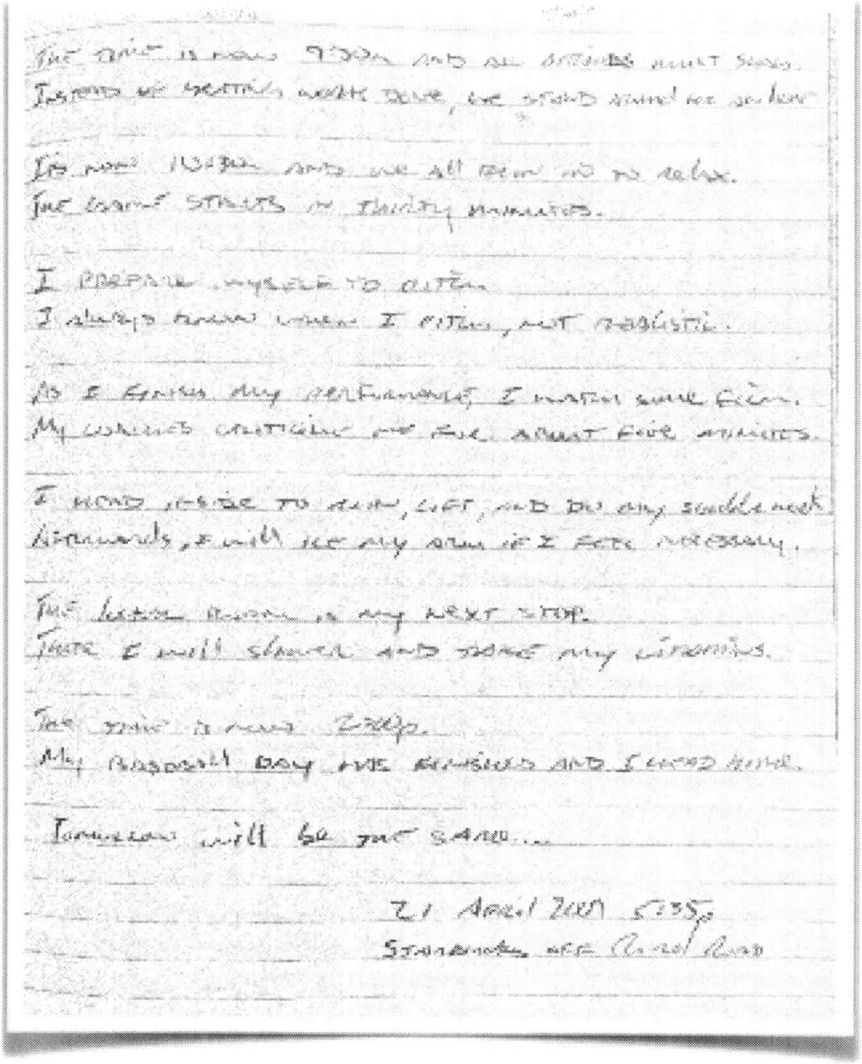

The time is now 9:30am and all athletes must stay.
Instead of getting work done, we stand around the locker.

It's now 12:30pm and we all begin to relax.
The game starts in thirty minutes.

I prepare myself to pitch.
I always know when I pitch, not [illegible].

As I finish my performance, I watch some film.
My coaches criticize me for about four minutes.

I head inside to run, lift, and do my shoulder work.
Afterwards, I will ice my arm if I feel necessary.

The locker room is my next stop.
There I will shower and take my vitamins.

The time is now 2:30p.
My baseball day has finished and I head home.

Tomorrow will be the same...

21 April 2009 5:35pm
Statement of [illegible]

6. The Last Decision

Date: April 29, 2009
Time: 8:45 PM
Location: Mesa, Arizona

"The Last Decision"

The feelings of,
The game I loved.
The summer air,
So dry and fair.

The leather ready,
The cotton fresh.
The ground just groomed,
The grass just edged.

You never know,
When you will go.
Don't try and think,
Don't turn to drink.

You see it so,
They come and go.
Once they knew,
Now out and blue.

The decision hard,

But some will make.
The ties they had,
The friends they made.

If they leave,
The game they'll watch.
The friends they had,
Those times not lost.

So when you choose,
Which road to take,
Make sure your mind,
Be free of angst.

Synopsis

This piece is about another player I played with who ultimately came to the conclusion that baseball was not his calling. This is sometimes a very hard decision for some because this is a sport that you feel you can do forever, but sometimes you come to the realization that you've hit your ceiling and you have maxed out your opportunity. He tried the best he could and worked harder than anyone I ever saw, but his vocation was not baseball so he moved on.

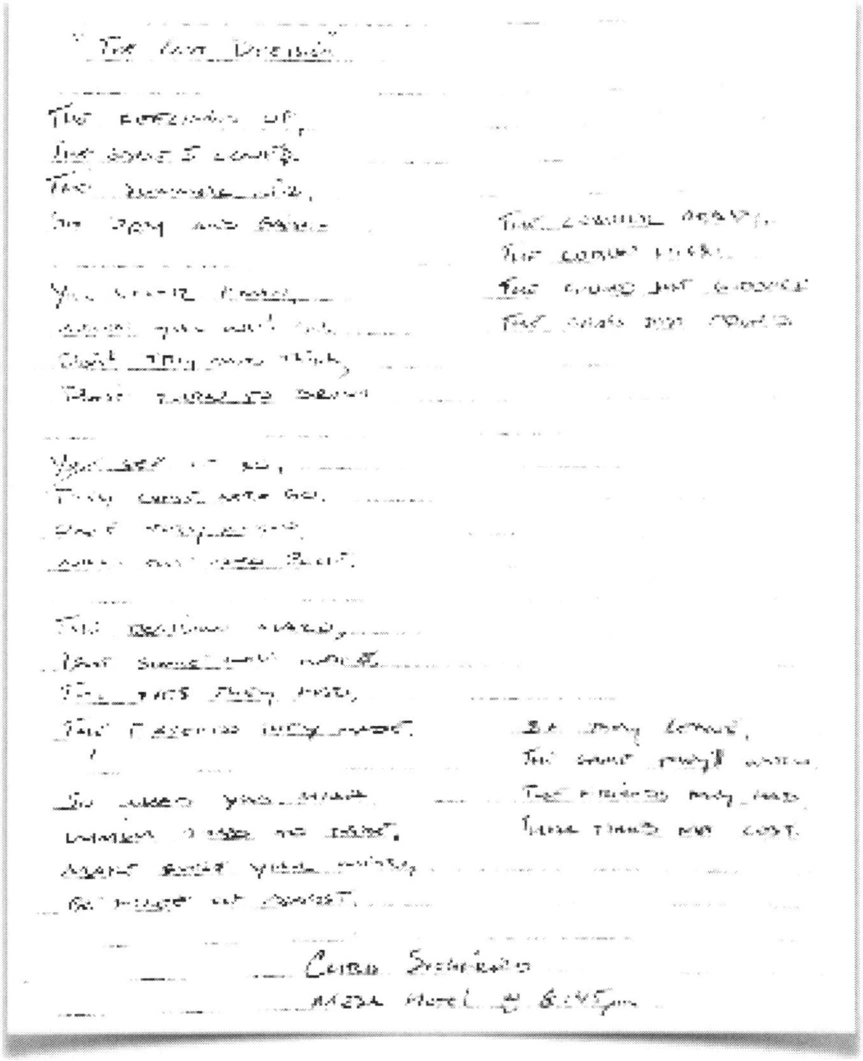

7. Easily Persuaded

Date: May 3, 2009
Time: 3:45pm
Location: Mesa, Arizona

"Easily Persuaded"

In a world full of greed,
It's hard not to give in.
The mind must be strong,
Harness the power within.

Everyday news full of rubbish,
People are running around with fear.
Fear for their lives, not thinking clearly,
Easily persuaded by the news they hear.

What happened to the thoughts and reflections?
Opinions formulated by personal obsession.
For things that effect their daily lives,
Be careful of listening to just one side.

So many things we don't understand,
The choices of those in command.
We once were told that things would change,
History is past don't look to blame.

So the next time you hear something of interest,

Listen closely to what is said.
Because in the end all sides unfolded,
The heart will decide where to begin.

Synopsis

This is a piece I wrote because of all that was happening in the world politically, religiously and on the baseball field. It is always important to read as much as you can in order to formulate your own opinions on any subject. Those who are readers are the enlightened one and are not so "easily persuaded" in life. They can think for themselves and make educated decisions that may not necessarily line up with the "masses," but are what is best at that time for them and the people around them. Don't give in to greed and gluttonous behavior of many, rather stay true to yourself and what your goals and aspirations are and "stay the course."

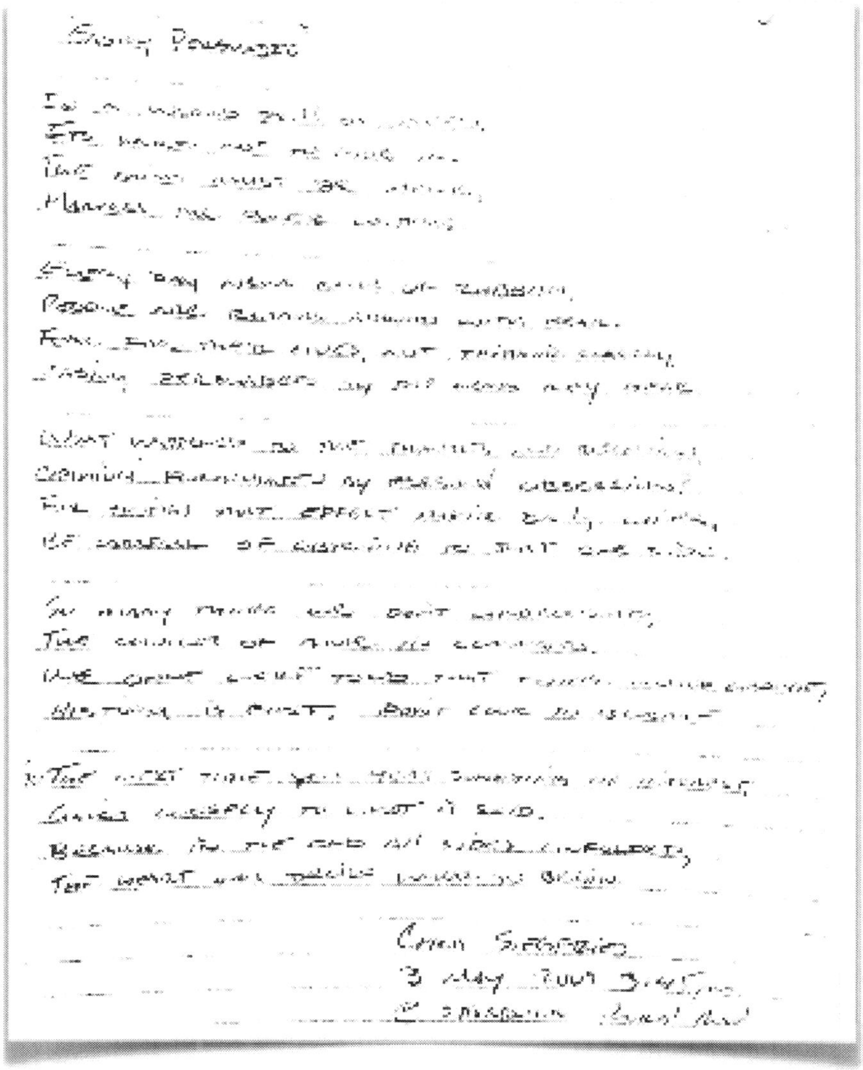

8. Waiting For The Call

Date: May 9, 2009
Time: 3:45 PM
Location: A Starbucks in Arizona

"Waiting for the Call"

He sits and wonders every day,
Not sure where he'll be come end of May.
But one thing he does understand,
Not even those above him know.

How can one have feelings?
Control out of his hands.
He waits and plays,
The best he can.

The call comes in,
The feelings strong,
All the work pays off,
Those days were long.

Now on the plane,
Next stop there he will play.
He's on the field,
But the mind still strays.

Back to when

The days so long,
He looks to the sky,
And thanks God he's gone.

Synopsis

Here is a piece that I wrote right after I got the call to move up another level. In baseball, life, and work you try to do the best you can and put all of your effort in your work to hopefully move up to another level or position. This piece is about all of the hard work I put into making it to the next level and some of the emotions that were involved when I ultimately got the call.

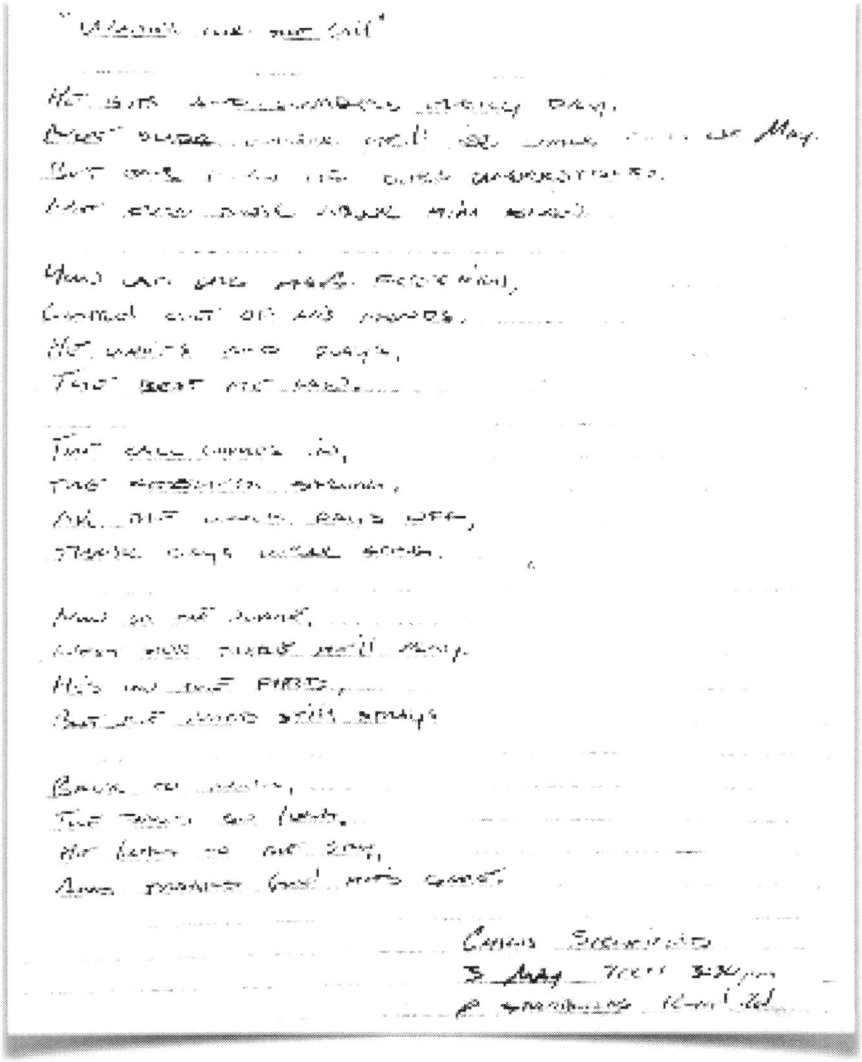

9. May 6

Date: May 6, 2009
Time: 4:00 PM
Location: Mesa, Arizona

"May Six"

The call came in and I was surprised,
All of these days with tired eyes.
My expectations kept up real high.
The emotions within me no need to cry.

I lay deep in sleep surrounded by water,
Not hearing the phone calls that truly matter.
My thoughts diverted by all this clatter,
The lawn chairs as noisy as falling ladders.

The message is such that my time is here,
Pack your bags, your locker be clear.
Tomorrow you travel away from here.
The friends you've made hold them dear.

Now to my mind and what is running,
All kinds of thoughts they don't stop coming.
Why should I go back to this place?
What is the answer? Your mechanics' changed.

Accept the call for life is challenging,

Small steps turn to big embrace the following.
Peoria bound, you've been there before.
This time is all business and nothing more.

Stay the course and the rest will follow.
Get comfortable with being uncomfortable.
Be happy with life and the progress you've made.
Never give up and you'll have your day!

Synopsis

When I wrote this poem, all I could think about was all of the training an hard work and support from family and friends - The day had finally come to where I was continuing my career and moving on to the next level.

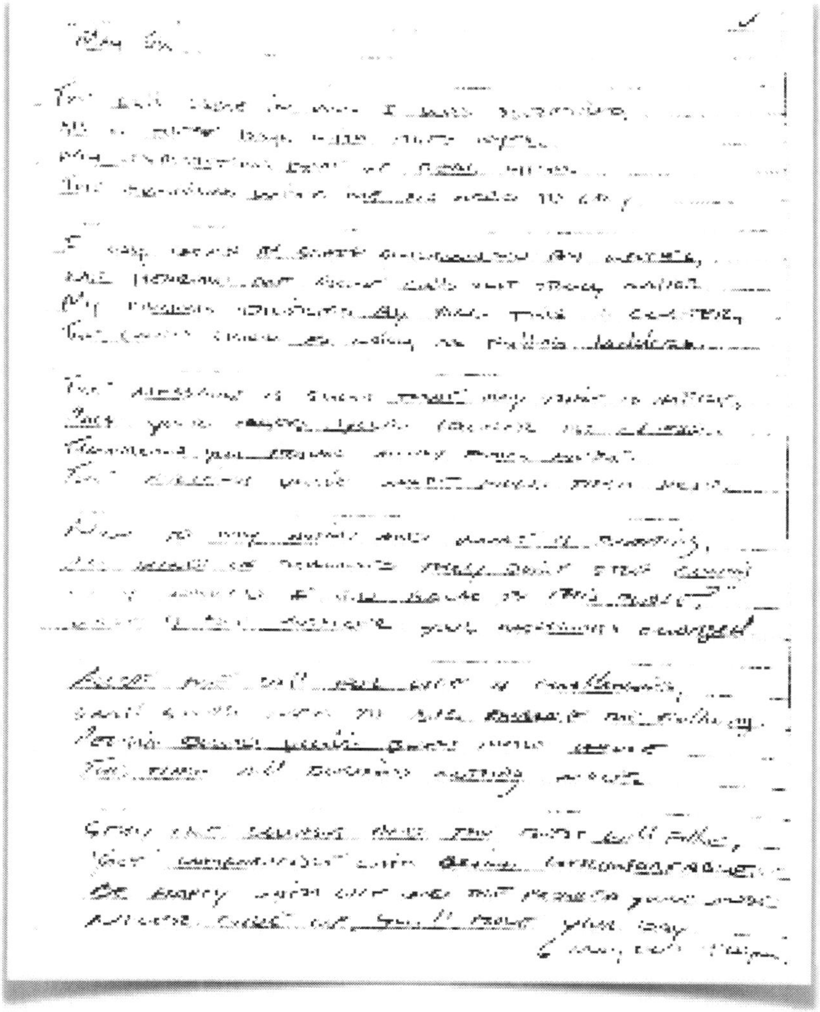

10. The Next Chapter

Date: May 8, 2009
Time: 1:20 PM
Location: Fort Wayne, Indiana

"The Next Chapter"

The park you will land from dry to damp air,
The feelings of discomfort you must bear.
Not because of the surroundings you're in,
But more from experience that one holds akin…

Experience that lasts for but only a few,
Memories engrained with each day a new.
For it is you who decides how you will respond,
Take each as a lesson to build upon.

This time is now different new chapter in hand,
It is he with the pen that shows much demand.
To call upon the new talents he's grown,
To write in that chapter to call his own.

Stay with the program the routines have been built,
They find solace in the hard times that will come about.
Stick to your instincts whenever in doubt,
For it is you that is present, here in the now.

Synopsis

This is another piece about the time I got called up to the next level, something I had been working towards for months. Enjoy.

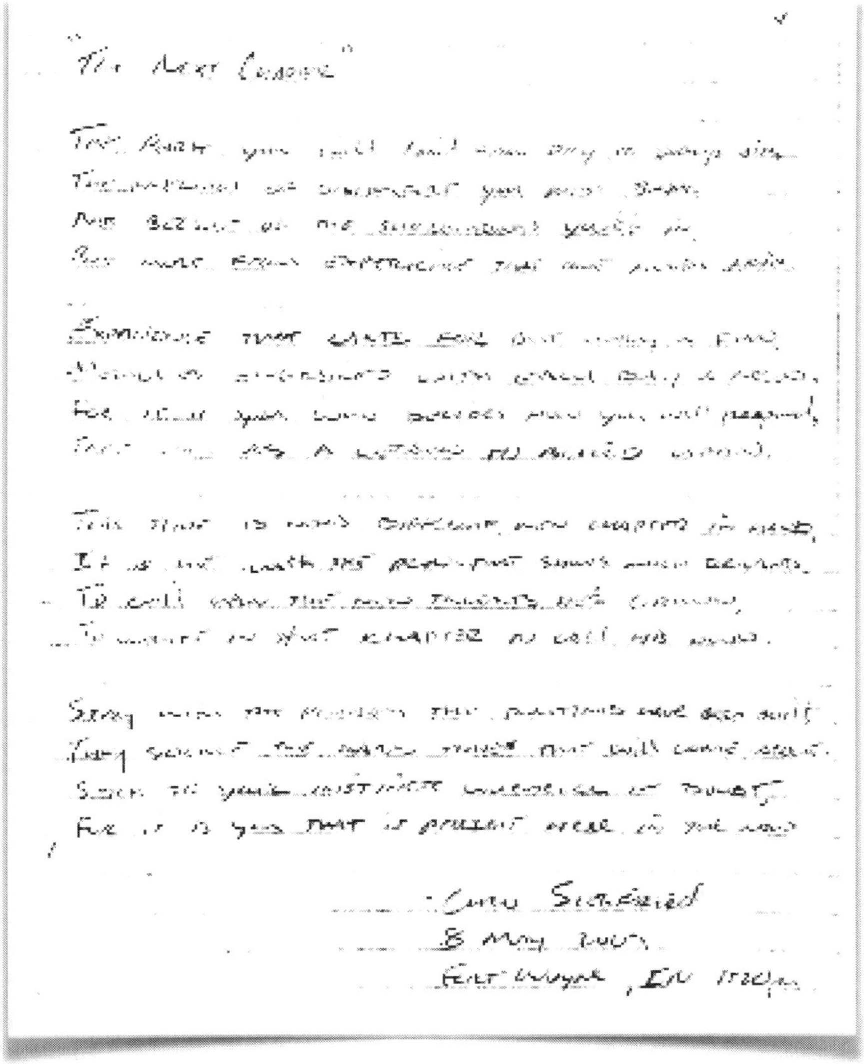

11. Raise a Toast

Date: May 13, 2009
Time: 11:47 PM
Location: Peoria, Illinois

"Raise a Toast!"

He's not perfect,
Mistakes he's made.
Sometimes regrets,
But fun times we made.

One or two, well maybe ten.
Drinks start slow,
Fast in the end.

Drank all the bottomless drinks,
All the girls that look, he winks.
Too quick to say hi and without a stammer,
He goes in for the kiss it doesn't matter.

One or two, well maybe ten.
Drinks start slow,
Fast in the end.

Lets go dance, a round on me.
One dance turns two, one round turns three.
The shoes come off George on and loud,

"The Race is On" boy make me proud!

One or two, well maybe ten.
Drinks start slow,
Fast in the end.

It's time to go head to the counter,
The bill needs be paid, $100 matters.
Bartender turns says one more round?
What the hell we'll have a crown.

One or two, well maybe ten.
Drinks start slow,
Fast in the end.

The lights are on time to cab home,
Hell I can't drive, but I'm not alone.
The ride seems long back seat so small,
She's on my neck lipstick and all!

One or two, well maybe ten.
Drinks start slow,
Fast in the end.
What time is it?
Oh hell, does it matter?
The one I love,
Says Johnny Walker.

One or two, well maybe ten.
I'm way too drunk,
Whiskey stronger in the end…

Synopsis

There are so many innuendos and nuances here. Where do I begin? First off, baseball was fun and I enjoyed meeting new people, but this is not a story about my experiences or myself. Rather, this is about THAT guy on the team that never sleeps, parties and still performs - not the way to go about the game but it happens all the time.

"One or two, well maybe ten. Drinks start slow, Fast in the end." This was a fun chorus, if you will, that I came up with describing an evening of minimal expectations but turned into an eventful night!

"George on and loud" is a reference to the late and great musician George Jones and his song "The Race is On." Country music if you are into that sort of thing.

I will let you decide for yourself what the rest means and where I was going with some of the stanzas.

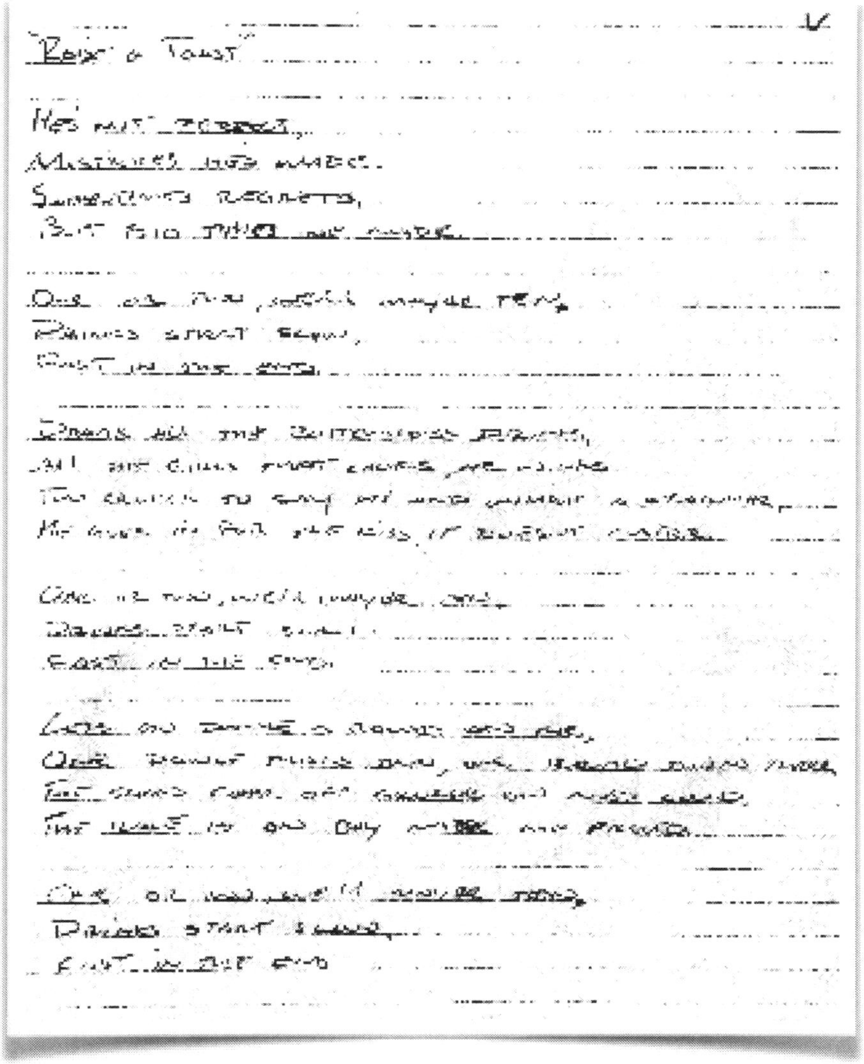

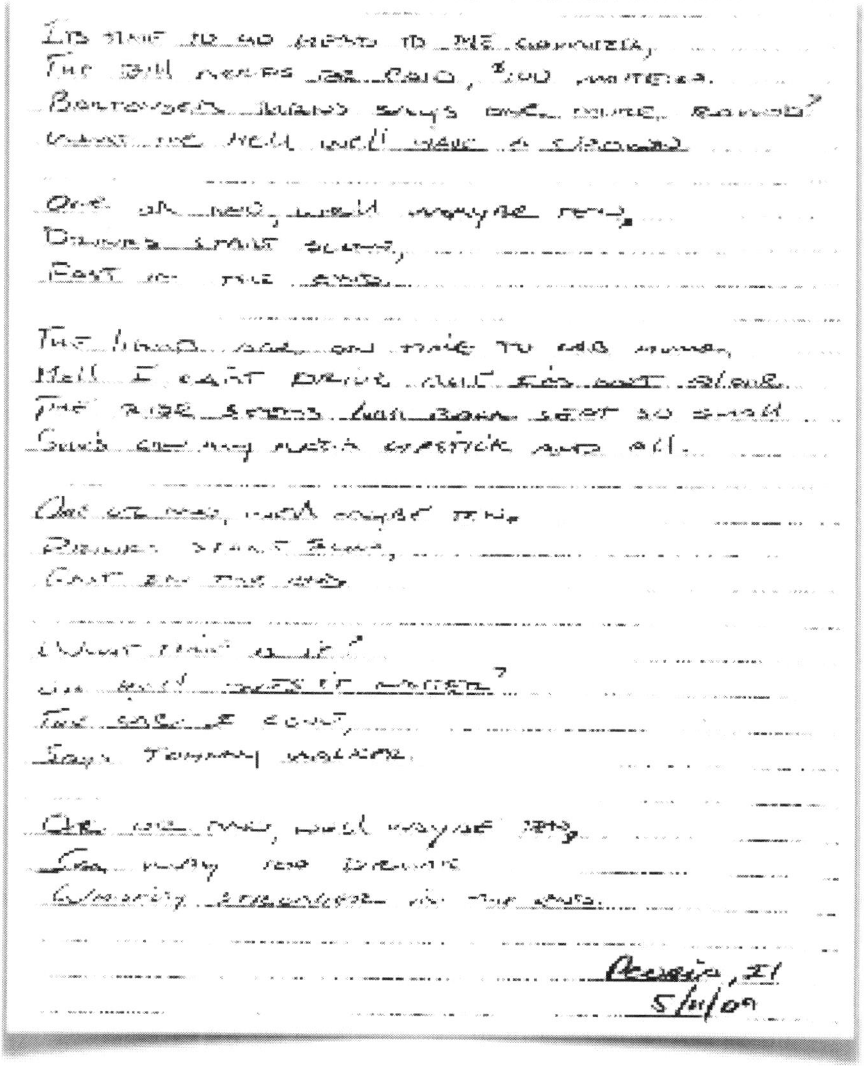
The bill needs to be paid, [illegible] no matter.
Bartender [illegible] says one more round?
What the hell we'll have [illegible]

One [illegible] well maybe ten,
[illegible]
[illegible] the end.

[illegible]
[illegible]
[illegible]
[illegible] and all.

One [illegible] well maybe ten,
[illegible]
[illegible] the end.

What time is it?
[illegible] does it matter?
[illegible]
Says Tommy [illegible]

One [illegible] well maybe ten,
[illegible]
[illegible] in the end.

[illegible], Il
5/11/09

12. Unpredictable Weather

Date: May 15, 2009
Time: 5:35 PM
Location: Peoria, Illinois

"Unpredictable Weather"

There's humor in the way the world goes,
One day comes sun, next day be snow.
But patterns there is not, make it hard to adapt,
Here come the clouds, the sun they will trap.

You woke up this morning,
Both birds and blue sky's,
Clouds on the horizon,
Mother nature will cry.

The rain has come and wet we all are,
The thunder and lightning seen from afar.
You run for cover rain jacket and all,
The wind now howling the branches all fall.

The soil now soaked and its thirst now quenched,
The ground all flooded, the rain it drenched.
What to expect but only the sun,
A picture so perfect a rainbow has come.

But here we wait for next weather adventure,
Only the jacket is of little or no avail.

The rain, no sun, well snow, maybe thunder,
Not up to us, Mother Nature prevails.

Synopsis

This is just a random poem I wrote about the changes in weather. I can not remember too well where my mind was, but enjoy it for what it is and draw some of your own conclusions.

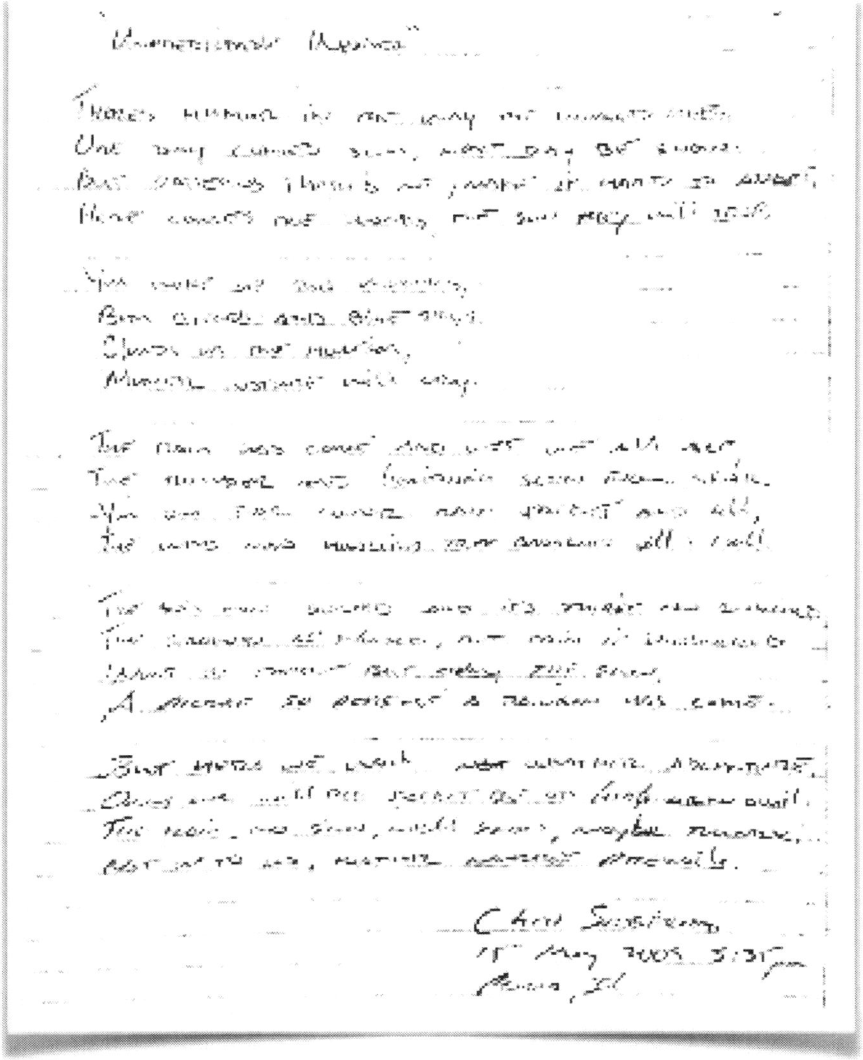

13. Your Life

Date: May 15, 2009
Time: 3:46 PM
Location: Starbucks in Peoria, Illinois

"Your Life"

We all will work,
One way or another.
But we must choose,
The thing we love.

Sometimes we are blinded by greed.
Sometimes we are blinded by perks.
But at the end of the day when we lay to rest,
Think of what you're doing and if it really works…for you.

Many people go around searching for that perfect job.
Many people settle with what they're doing.
Why should we settle with something we don't want?
Why not put social pressures aside and do what's best?

Life is too short to be unhappy.
If you dread waking up in the morning, rethink.
Look yourself in the mirror, be honest.
Are you doing what you want with your life?

It is your life not the life of others.
Your decisions ultimately affect you.
Be happy with your daily activities.
Don't be a puppet to clichés.

Synopsis

This is about finding your vocation and being happy with what you ultimately choose to do in life. Far too many people gripe and complain about the perils of work and how they wish they could be doing something else. Go after that "something else" and do it if it would make you happy because we were only given so much time on this Earth to do the best we can and make a difference. Be happy and do the best you can at whatever it is you do and if along the way you can make a difference, do so.

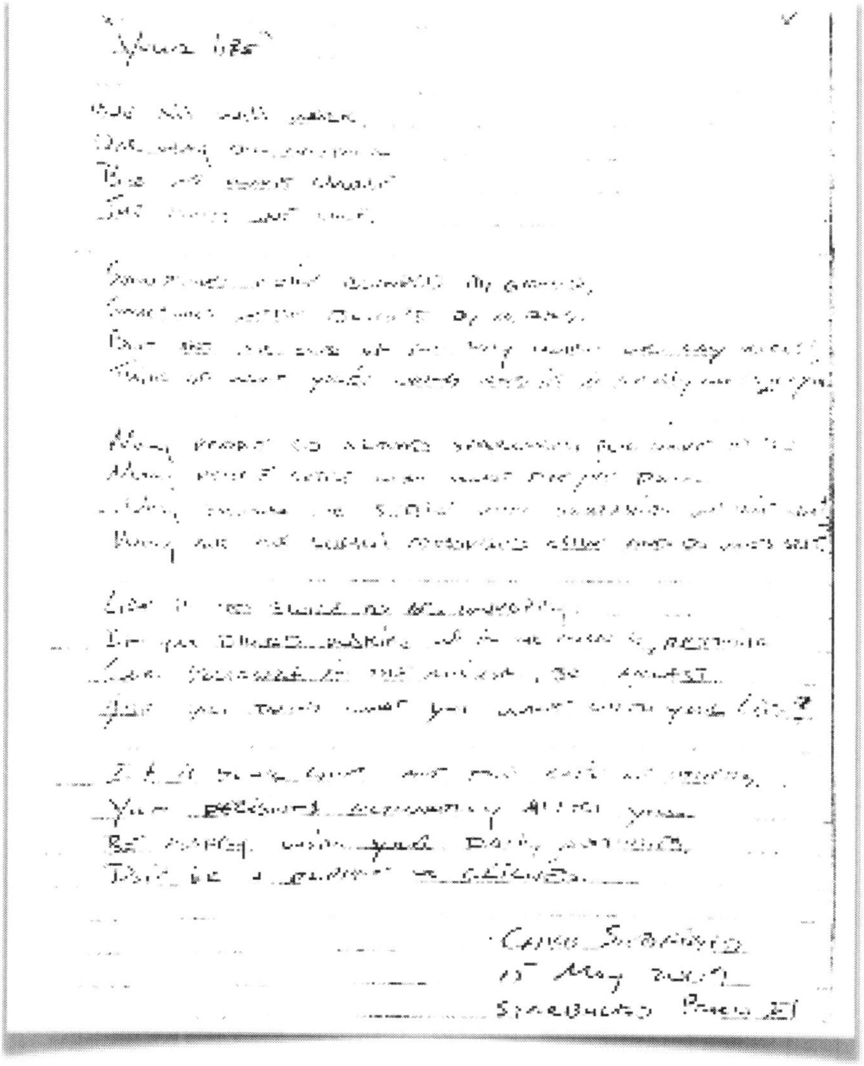

14. Silence

Date: May 28, 2009
Time: 1:40 PM
Location: Peoria, Illinois

"Silence"

The sound of silence one says is peaceful.
But what about when you are around,
People sharing different stories,
You in the background nowhere to be found.

Strongly judged when one does listen,
This silence not quite understood.
Is it because the mindless thinking,
Or for the arrogance many pursue?

The mind will wonder when alone to long,
Fueled by the silence ever so strong.
Surrounded by those not familiar with,
Behaviors developed, stay humble within.

For when the sound of silence breaks,
May come too soon or long may take.
Remember back three lines before,
Keep silent within, loud noises adored.

Synopsis

Here we have an interesting outlook on the behavior of those I was around in the clubhouse. You see, when you are around the same group of guys for seven months, you start to notice certain habits and tendencies.

The people who get tired of the "grind" usually start to become rather irritated and have short tempers. The guys who keep to themselves continue to stay quiet and do their own thing. There is nothing wrong with that, but sometimes people don't take a liking to doing your own thing and staying private.

Line seven is not meant to be a poke at the abrasive behaviors I was around. Rather, over time the conversation that took place was empty. Some of those in the locker room decided to keep to themselves during these times trying not to get wrapped up in the unruly behavior of others around them. This did not go over so well with some of those who were loud and outspoken, sometimes causing drama. "Behaviors developed, stay humble within" is a line meant to point out that it is ok to keep to yourself and to not get caught up in the behavior of those around you.

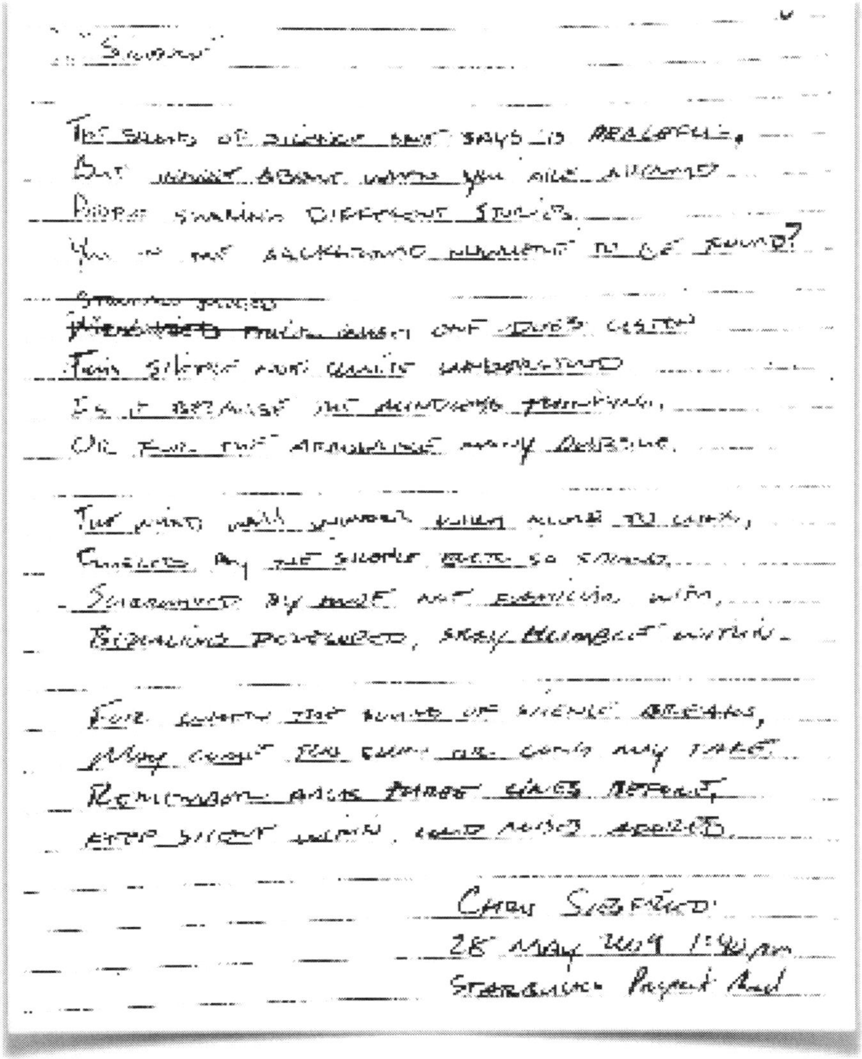

15. Life

Date: May 31, 2009
Time: 12:15 AM
Location: Midland, Michigan

"Life"

At first you think that everything's fine,
Losing track of those important, not in mind.
Then reality sets in when you get the call,
One not quite close but family lost it all.

Not too certain of what did happen,
But understand the value of,
Life and all of its surroundings,
Don't take for granted the ones you love.

With everyone there is a purpose,
Many search whole lives to find.
Some find comfort in the hands
Of the one Creator truly divine.

Ask yourself if you are happy,
With decisions made in days passed.
If unsure of where you're headed,
Look to God, not afraid to ask.

If you have doubt of what you're doing,

Whatever part in life you're at.
Remember to keep things in perspective,
For someone else may have it bad.

For when your day comes most do not know,
Be at peace with all, your heart can grow.
Love family, friends, God and all the like,
You'll feel complete with your own life.

Synopsis

The first stanza speaks to a family member of mine that passed away. This family member was very dear to me and cared for me, but our communication slipped and before I knew it, they had passed on. I was very upset and regretted the fact that we did not stay in touch as much as I would have enjoyed. It made me reflect on what I was doing with my life.

This person enjoyed life to the fullest and did their best to be the best at what they did. I wanted to be like that person and so I decided to push harder and work to be the best I could be at my God-given talent. It also made me realize that I needed to be thankful for my gifts because at any moment they could be taken away from me. I had to remember to not take them for granted because someone else may not have the same opportunity and ability and I needed to be thankful for my blessings.

"Love family, friends, God and all the like,
You'll feel complete with your own life."

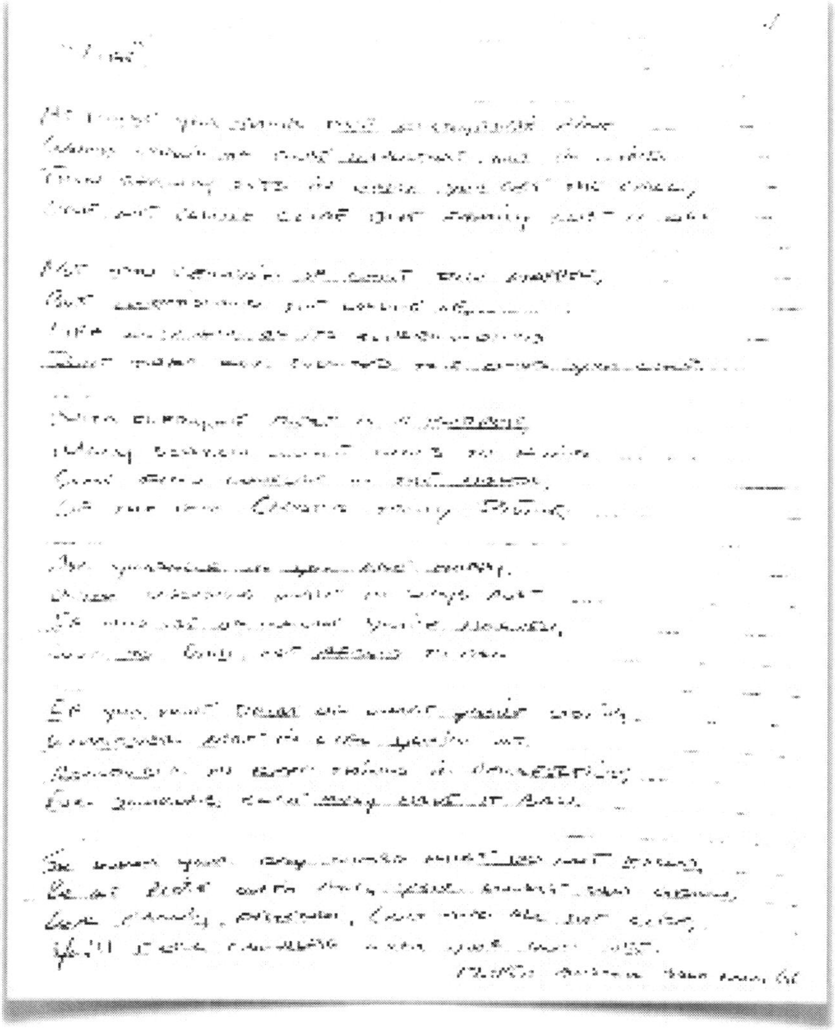

16. Smell This

Date: June 12, 2009
Time: 2:45 PM
Location: Clinton, Iowa

"Smell This"

Can you imagine a place,
Where the food you just can't taste.
Not because the lack of flavor,
More for reasons that fill the air.

Some can stand outside with ease,
Others sit inside displeased.
Then there are those who can do without,
Both inside and outside there is no doubt.

Stop and think just for one second,
There are those who call this home.
But dog food permeates the air around us,
Lets just say "to each is own."

Back up, rewind, let us start over,
I'm sure there is something 38 sq. mi. has to offer.
We know its not food or casinos full of smoke.
Stay here too long and premature you'll croak.

One chance has been given now second I write,
Information for those who just might,

Get offered a job at the Purina dog tower,
You'll wake up each morning and forget the flowers.

Synopsis

As I was writing this poem I was sitting in a Super 8 hotel in Clinton, Iowa. This was meant to be a fun off the cuff piece. I don't know if you have ever been to Clinton, but the entire small, Midwest city has a very unique smell. When the wind is blowing just right, it doesn't matter if you are inside your house, hotel, car or outside, if feels as if your head is in a giant bag of freshly made dog food. Some may like this smell, others… not so much.

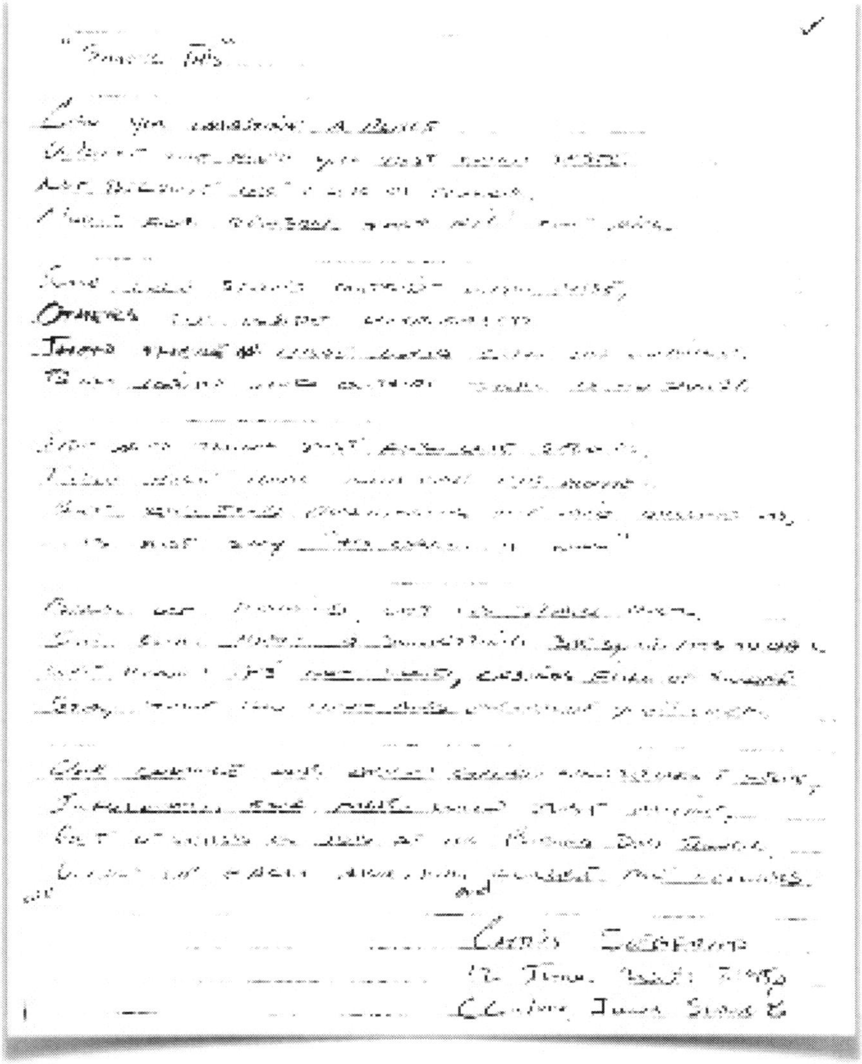

17. The Loneliest Walk

Date: June 20, 2009
Time: 10:15 PM
Location: Appleton, Wisconsin

"The Loneliest Walk"

As the end draws near,
Intensity, the crowd is all you here.
But not when one is in the moment,
Rather on the sideline in the clear.

The pressure mounts but train you do,
For the time that comes, nothing is new.
The call comes in we're up and ready,
Change of pace don't keep it steady.

Walk to the mound not lonely yet,
Confidence and the ball we get.
From outings that oh did end so well,
The coach is proud just give it hell.

One pitch is good another low,
The game not fair, the way it goes.
It's one and one the ball in play,
Just out of reach the guy is safe.

Now man on first the game is close,

The score in favor of not the host.
Tides have turned run has come in,
Now the game closer then begin.

Momentum swing not for the better,
Into the 9th the crowd is ever,
So loud the noises from within,
Stadium erupting rally begins.

Pitcher surrounded all bases full,
Home is the only place to go.
The ball in play but bobbled slow,
Play at the plate here comes the throw…

Opposition rushes the field.
Pitcher tried not to yield,
The winning run but team at fault,
Effort not from all confident, much doubt.

The tunnel the next place to go,
Unfortunately no light does glow.
Only light that comes from within,
The room that fills with wounded kin.

Even though the walk feels long,
As if you crossed the desert strong.
With winds howling straight on in,
Sand in face and comfort thin.

You pitched your best things unfold not true,
Nothing new you're so used to,
The game and all its failure brings,
New strength for which to build and sing.

The hardest thing dealt with day in and out,
The failure that comes in no doubt.
But how one truly responds to,
The games' last outing, its up to you.

Synopsis

Follow me as I walk you through this poem in its entirety. This was a game that left an impression in my mind. It was the bottom of the eighth and I was called in to pitch in a one run ball game with a man on second. These are the moments I trained for everyday. I wanted to be in the pressure situations when the game was on the line because it was an adrenaline rush and it meant that my coach had faith in me to get the job done.

The first batter came up and squeezed a ball just passed the middle infielder. It was not a good hit, but very well placed and one run scored from second to tie the game up. On into the ninth inning and the game and it's momentum got out of hand. A pitch here and a hit there, an error and all of a sudden the bases were loaded with two outs.

I made a pitch down and inside and jammed the batter but he fought it off and blooped it over the second baseman's head. The game was over and there was nothing I could do at that point but watch the opposition rush the field. It was a hard loss because it was a team loss. We had a few close plays, a few errant plays and a few poorly placed pitches that got hit to holes in the field where no one was.

You can read into the remainder of the poem to get the gist of how I felt. In the game of baseball you have to have a short term memory and be able to not carry your thoughts or previous performances into your next outing.

The title comes from the time I had to walk from the mound, through the dugout and into the what seemed to be the darkest tunnel with no light at the end. After some time and contemplation passed, I moved on and quickly forgot what had happened because I knew I would be in that situation again.

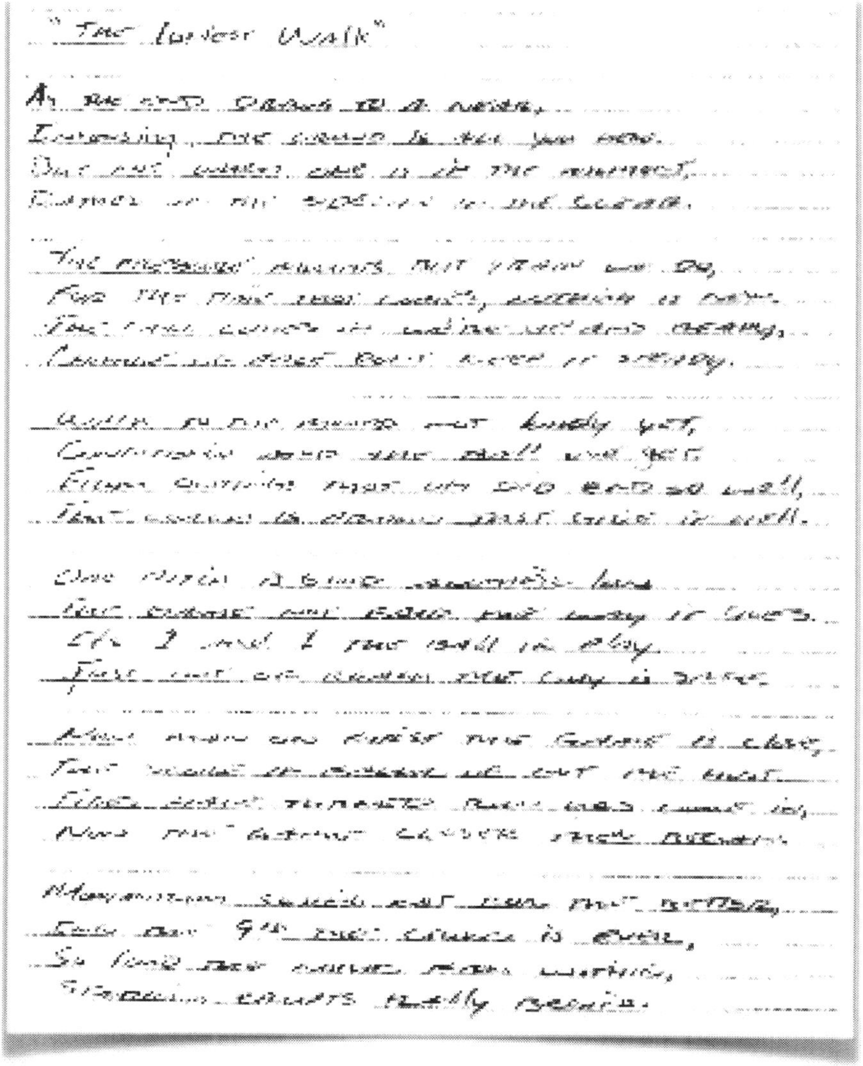

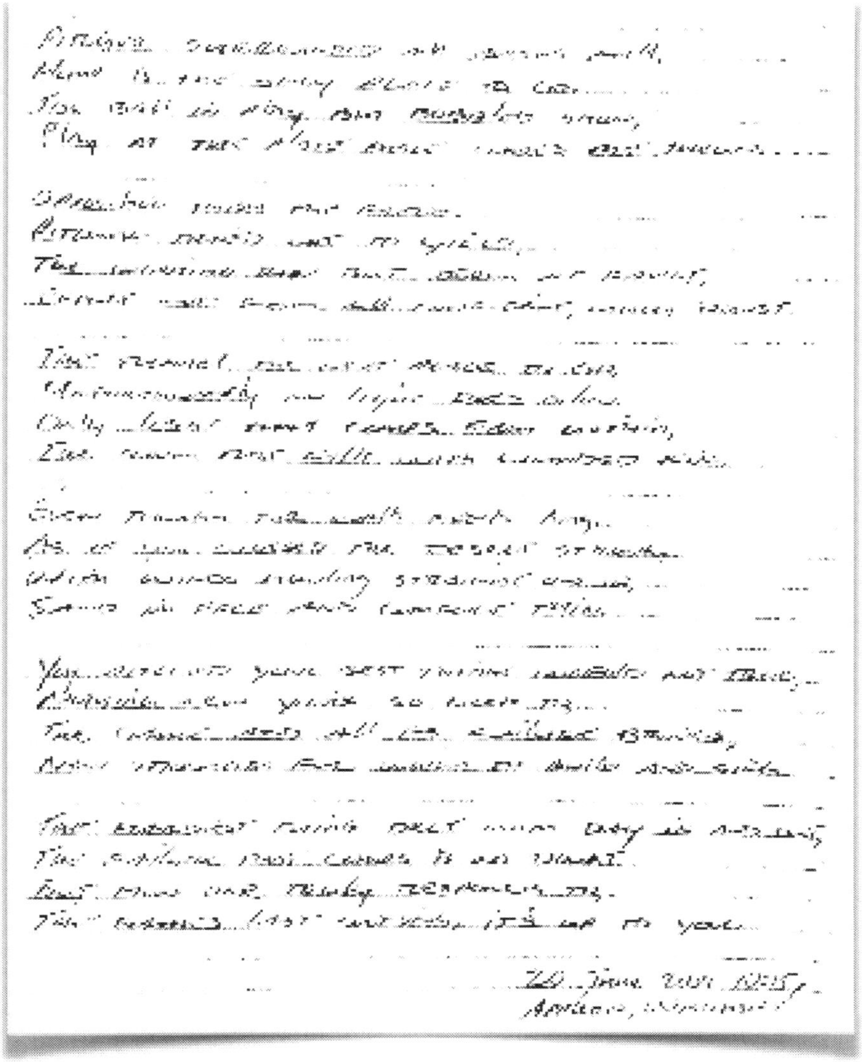

18. Dan's Release

Date: July 12, 2009
Time: 12:45 AM
Location: Peoria, IL

"Dan's Release"

There will come a time when your number is called,
And how you react will be up to you.
There are many options truth be told,
Stand up and be strong is all you can do.

This time it was red, the tag in your locker,
But it may very well be a blessing in disguise.
Do you attack the gift you've been given,
The ability that once brought you ninety-five?

Your training is thorough,
Your mind ever so strong,
Your drive is forever,
Your chase may only last so long.

Whichever you decide we support you completely,
This is your path and its up to you.
If baseball is the thing you want the most,
Then stay the course, kick but like you do.

Synopsis

This is a story of a friend of mine who's baseball career didn't ultimately pan out the way he expected it to or wanted it to because of unforeseen circumstances/ injuries. Dan was given the opportunity to play professional baseball and gave it everything he had. He was the first in the gym in the morning and the last to leave, getting better in the batting cages and on the field, oh, and had the magic ability of throwing a baseball ninety-five miles per hour. Unfortunately, a few injuries sidelined him long enough that he ultimately was faced with a decision of continuing the pursuit, or trying new endeavors. The baseball community, or at least my tight-knit group of friends, supported Dan and all of his decisions and are happy to see his successes continue in other aspects of his life now outside of baseball.

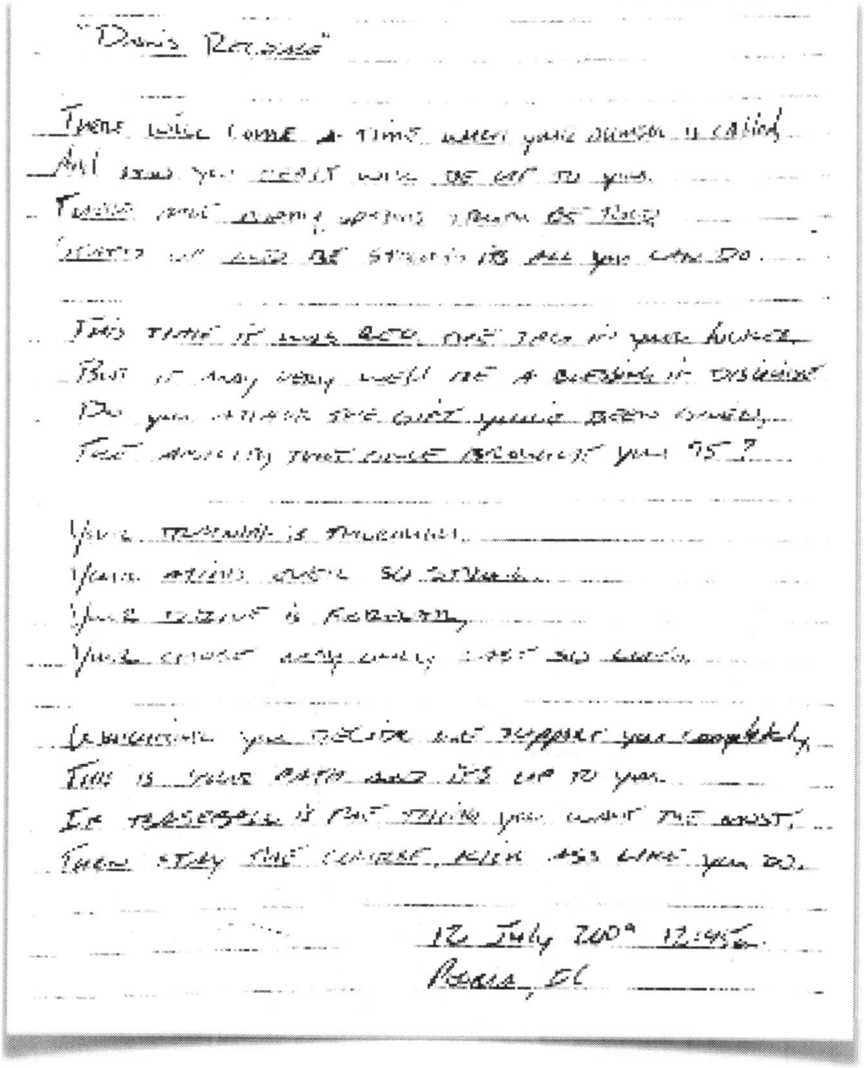

"Dan's Release"

There will come a time when your number is called
And [illegible] your [illegible] will be [illegible] to you.
[illegible]
[illegible] all you can do.

This time it [illegible] in your honor
But it may very well be a blessing in disguise
Do you think the [illegible] you've been [illegible]...
That [illegible] that [illegible] brought you [illegible]?

Your [illegible] is [illegible],
Your [illegible] so [illegible]...
Your [illegible] is [illegible]
Your [illegible] so [illegible],

[illegible] you [illegible] and support you completely,
This is your path and it's up to you.
If [illegible] is [illegible] you want the most,
Then stay the course, kick ass like you do.

12 July 200[illegible] 12:45 [illegible]
[illegible], FL

19. The Absence of Time

Date: July 19, 2009
Time: 1:30 PM
Location: Clinton, Iowa

"The Absence of Time"

There goes the cliché where time is of the essence,
But synonymous this will not be.
For the absence of time is day after day,
Start on the next line, the describing will be.

Some days may run long,
While others seem to short.
For baseball is the life we choose,
Repetition, the name of the game.

We go to the field to practice the profession,
Some people would rather just sit at home.
Confused as to why they are told what to do,
Yet all will tell you it's their obsession that holds true.

Time is not spent on productive matters,
Rather wasted on these mindless things.
The stereotype of baseball and meatheads,
The language spoken not soft and would ring…

Loud in the ears of those who would listen,

Conversations that take place during the day.
The locker room filled with unruly behavior,
All of these players with hopes that someday…

Their dreams will be answered at the top they will play,
But work too hard their mind does stray.
To things they'd rather do with their time,
Not focused on baseball but life in the limelight.

Arrive at the field and hang you will do,
With all of this free time it is up to you.
Some will work harder then ever before,
Usually those guys are the ones who want it more.

Then there are those who would rather chat,
About last night, all the bars they were at.
The girls they met and drinks they drank,
All crash in the morning, hydration it takes…

To wake them up but only their minds,
For the rest of them are all lost with the time.
They spent all night up and drank until four,
Only to stop, for the door is open no more.

Oh but you here a gasp of relief,
For the rain in the forecast brings disbelief.
Those that were drunk happier then ever,
Now get to go home and enjoy this weather.

But the guys at the park still wanting it bad,
Continue to train, it's all that they have.
The strength to go on no matter the delay,
For tomorrow will challenge the fallen today.

So next time you question the time you are given,
Remember time lost you cannot get back.
For when you time has run out and your bag in hand,
Don't make it you who took the number off you back.

Synopsis

This piece seems to be rather long. Enjoy it for what it is and see if you can find any metaphors and/or any hidden messages within.

I will give you one hidden message that I placed between the lines:
Whatever it is you find yourself doing, your calling if you will, give it everything you have so that when your time is over you can look back and be happy with yourself and the effort you put forth. Do not regret what you did and always try to do your best! Whatever it is you may do, you will look back and think about all the times you could have done this or that. Don't look back and have any regrets; look back and be happy with all of your decisions and hard work!

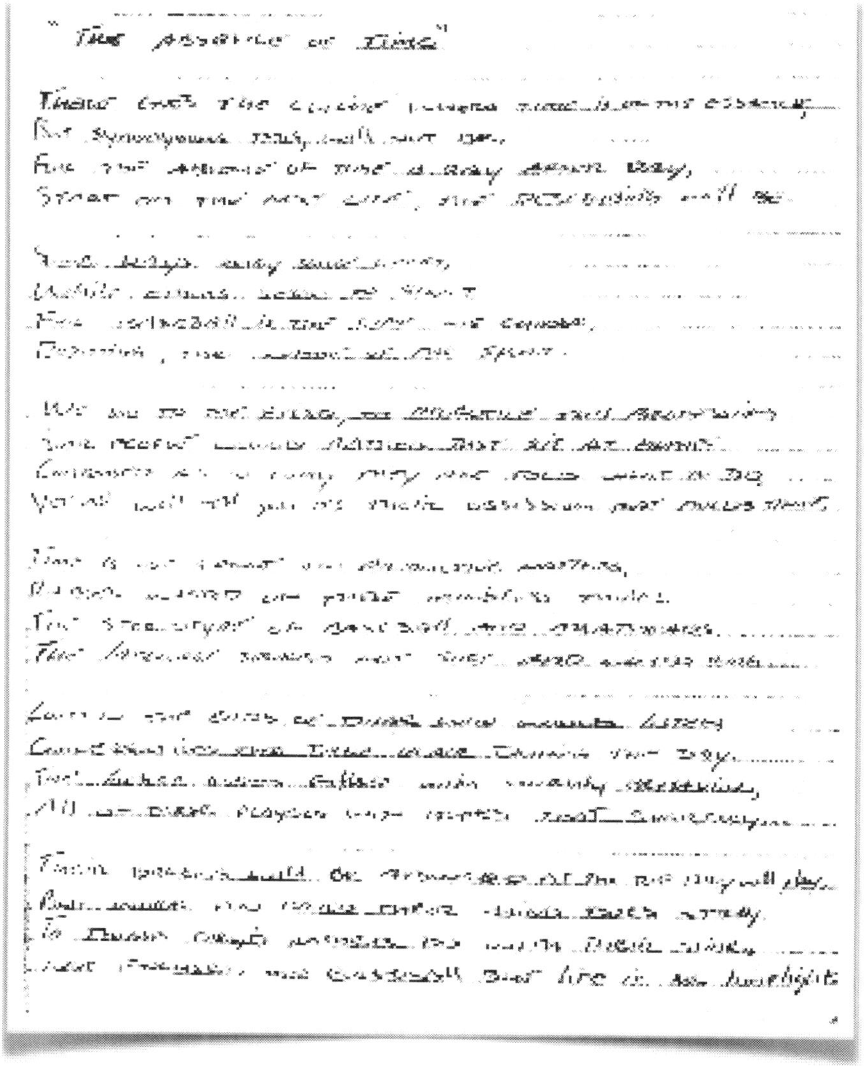

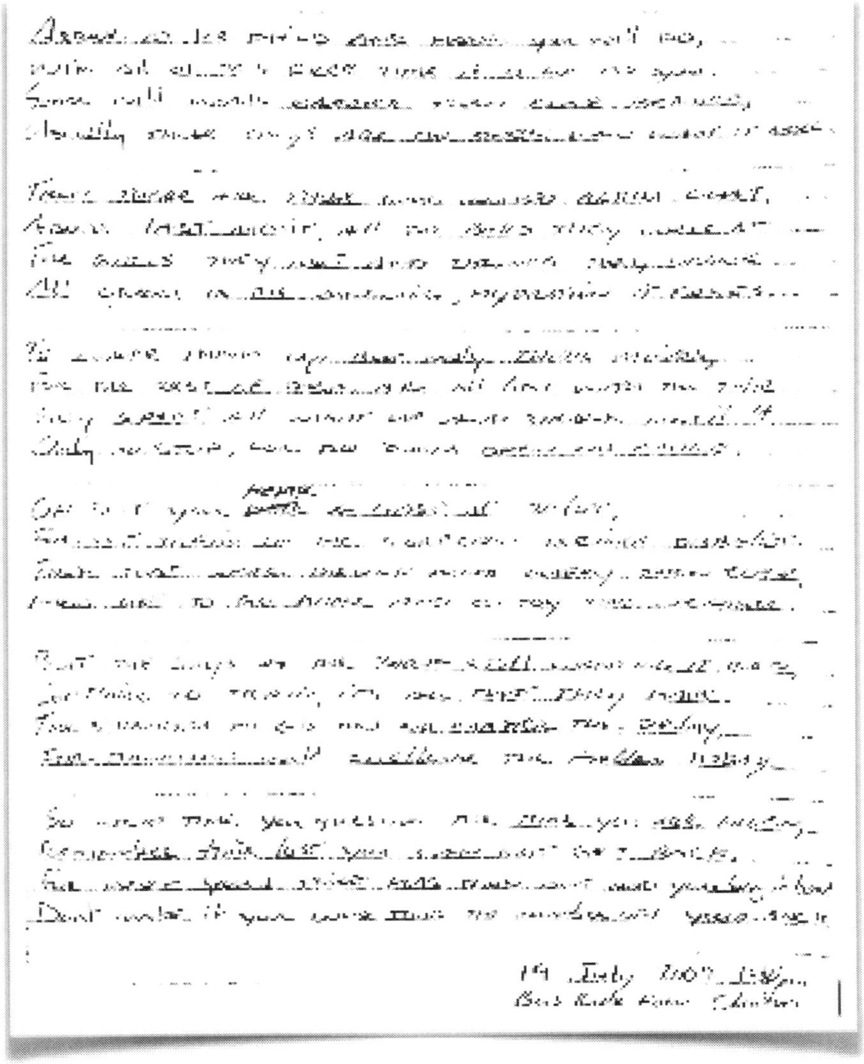

20. As it Peers

Date: July 29, 2009
Time: 1:30 PM
Location: Dayton, Ohio

"As it Peers"

As it stands there alone it bares much weight,
For the time has been long and the night is too late.
One does not expect the outcome that happened,
But controls almost nothing and leaves it to fate.

Its surroundings are empty but strong as they stand,
For they represent the perfect hand.
What all men train and strive for each day,
This perfect outcome all want to taste.

It continues to burn a hole so deep,
Ones' eyes can't help but to stare directly.
For the feelings that go along with one instance,
Will last forever but the mind must not be steady.

The instance may rise again and again,
The one that lasts has the strongest mind.
Recognizes defeat and understands there is failure,
But continues to strive for the odds he'll beat!

Synopsis

This is a very unique piece of writing for me. There are a lot of hidden metaphors and innuendos buried within the lines. If you understand the game of baseball, you'll understand what I mean.

"As it stands there alone it bares much weight, For the time has been long and the night is too late." Here I am referring to that one run I allowed in a potential no hitter I pitched in. "It stands there alone and bares much weight…" is referring to the fact that on the scoreboard the 1 is surrounded by 0s and the weight it bares is that of a loss because we lost that game 1-0.

I go on to talk about how it is hard to get over such defeat, but it is important to have a short-term memory and recognize that defeat will happen, but learning from that experience will give me the strength to overcome that situation when it arises again. In baseball you always get the chance to prove yourself in the same situation as before…it must be the baseball gods forcing us to beat the odds!

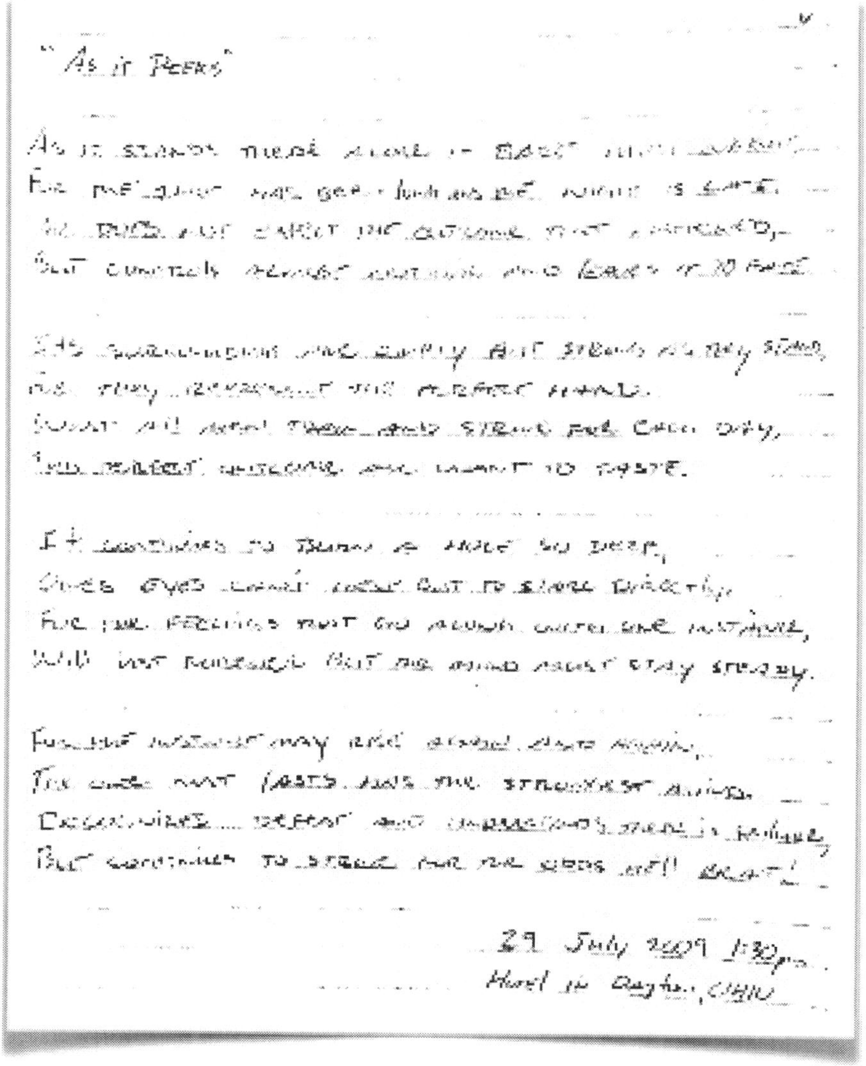

"As it Peers"

[illegible]

21. The Lost Inning

Date: July 31, 2009
Time: 2:15 AM
Location: South Bend, Indiana

"The Lost Inning"

Every day you prepare for the outing,
Not quite sure when it will be.
But preparation keeps you busy,
Even when rain is strong as can be.

You wait your turn like all else do,
Then pen is fresh all arms are new.
Ready to pitch each day through and threw,
Keeping your mind fresh is up to you.

For your day will come when you least expect,
The sun is out, the rain is next.
The starter in but only for a few,
Rules keep him grounded, the ball's for you.

Uncertain as what to expect,
Rain delay is all that's next,
9:10 to 20 pushed back so much,
Umpire not to quick to rush…

The call because the stands are full,

With nine thousand here it's never dull.
But rain does fill the radar whole,
The game be played in rain or snow.

You warm up for the game you love,
Just as if it were still sunny.
Not too much feel for the rain stays strong,
Keep your pace quick and steady.

Go into the game ready to pitch,
But rain still has its way with nature.
The ball is wet and ground too slick,
Strikes must be thrown its all you can control.

The inning goes not quite as planned,
But nonetheless zero still stands.
The other team unable to score,
The game still stands same as before.

Here comes the rain now harder then ever,
With just two outs the game is called!
The game and all its unruly weather,
Chiefs still on top but postponed be told.
For the inning pitches is all well and good,
But does not count but for personal pleasure.
The arm felt good few pitches thrown,
But none will stand on the record.

The inning's lost in the delay of game,
Due to all this pounding rain.
Next stop will be but not the same,
For forecast does not call for rain.

The way you pitched is quality still,
You gave your team the chance to win!
Every time you go back for more,
Make sure you are completely locked in!

Synopsis

This piece is about the inning I pitched in Dayton, Ohio that ultimately did not count because the game was suspended due to bad weather. We never made up that game or continued where we left off because we had no time to do so in our 140 game schedule that summer.

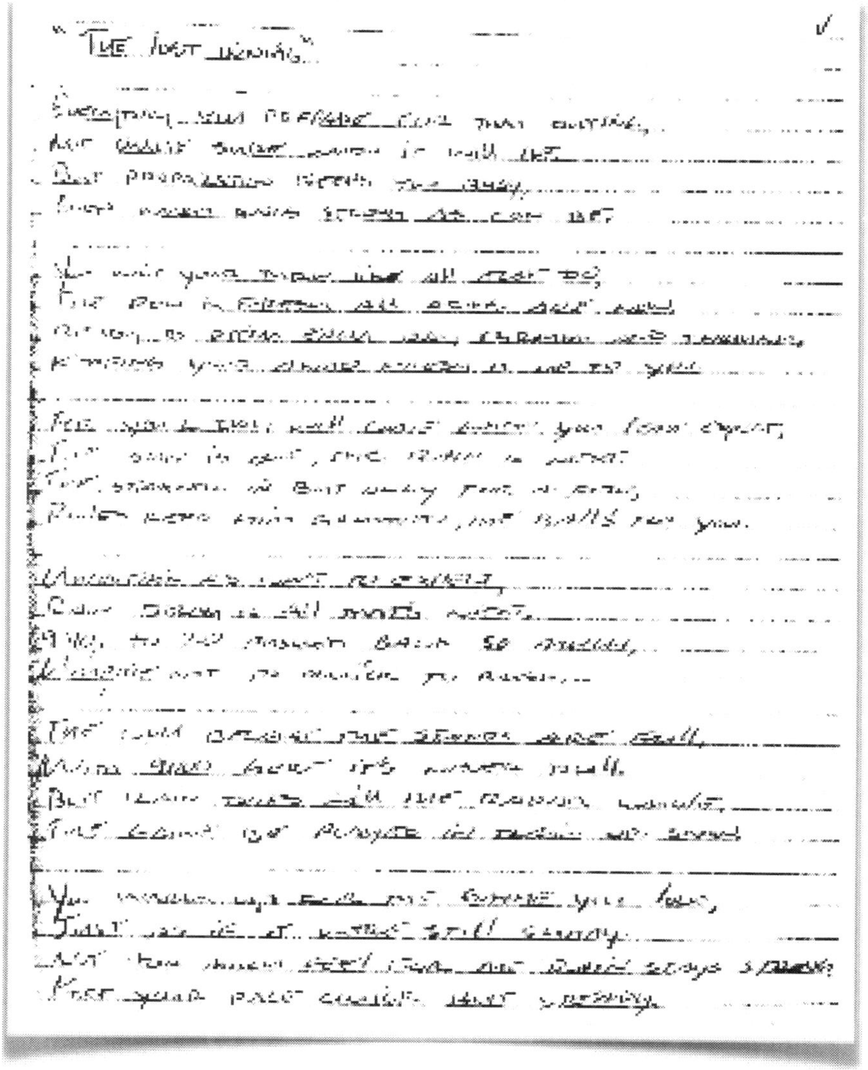

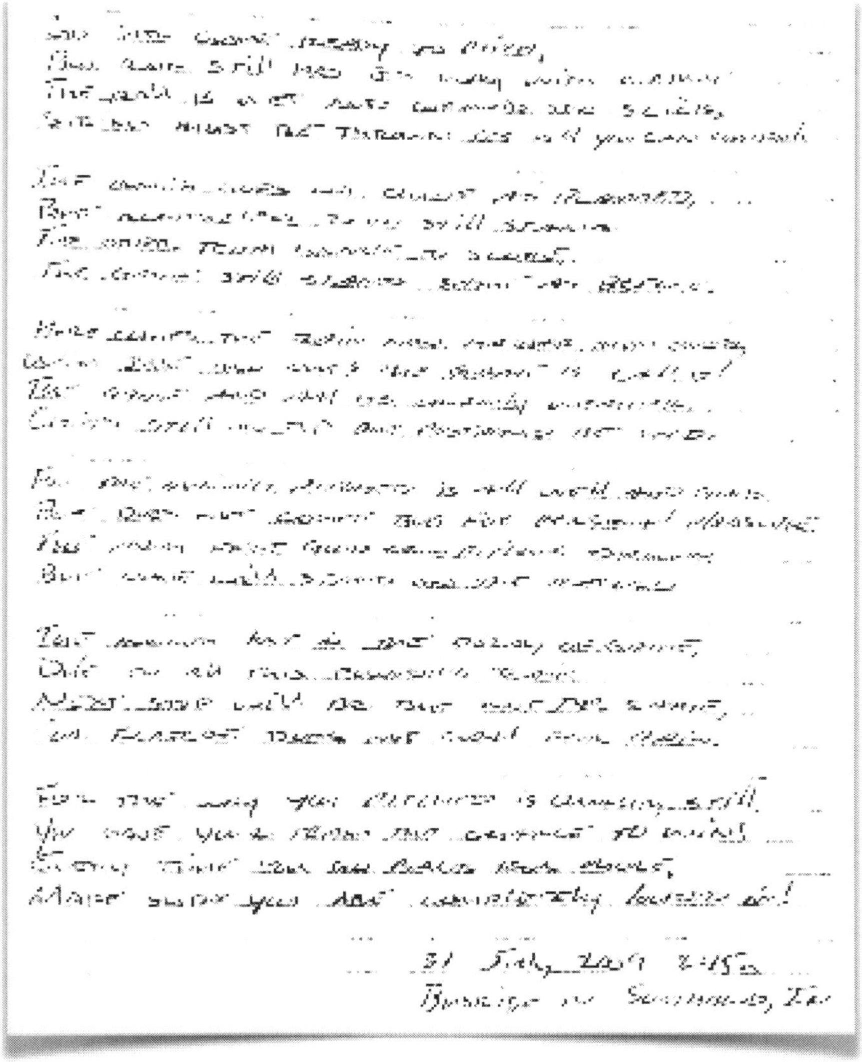

22. August First

Date: August 1, 2009
Time: 9:45 AM
Location: Detroit, MI

"August First"

As I sit in this airport air,
All types of emotions so hard to bear.
The destination and time spent there,
For not too long, but short is fare.

As I depart some will follow,
But reasons not the same as mine.
For I head to this sunny state for work!
Others all have beach in mind.

As my emotions begin to stir,
The mind so easily thrown off course.
For at least I have my goal and purpose,
This will help me stay the course.

For in this sport only one thing is wanted,
Wining is all they care about.
The distractions that lie within your head,
Are of now concern without a doubt.

As I sit in this airport air,

All types of emotions so hard to bear.
The destination and time spent there,
For not too long, but short is fare.

Synopsis

Here I describe the feelings of getting the call to move up to the next level in my baseball career. It is interesting to think that the other people in the airport have no idea why I am on the same plane as they are and I don't know their stories, but we are all moving forward in life.

The third stanza I am describing different distractions that happen during a young minor leaguer's career and the importance of how we have to keep in mind why we are playing and what we are playing for – the opportunity to play in the Big Leagues some day. That goal of mine helped me stay the course when so many distractions and obstacles were thrown my way. While it didn't ultimately work out, I can proudly say that I am happy with the effort I put forth in my pursuit.

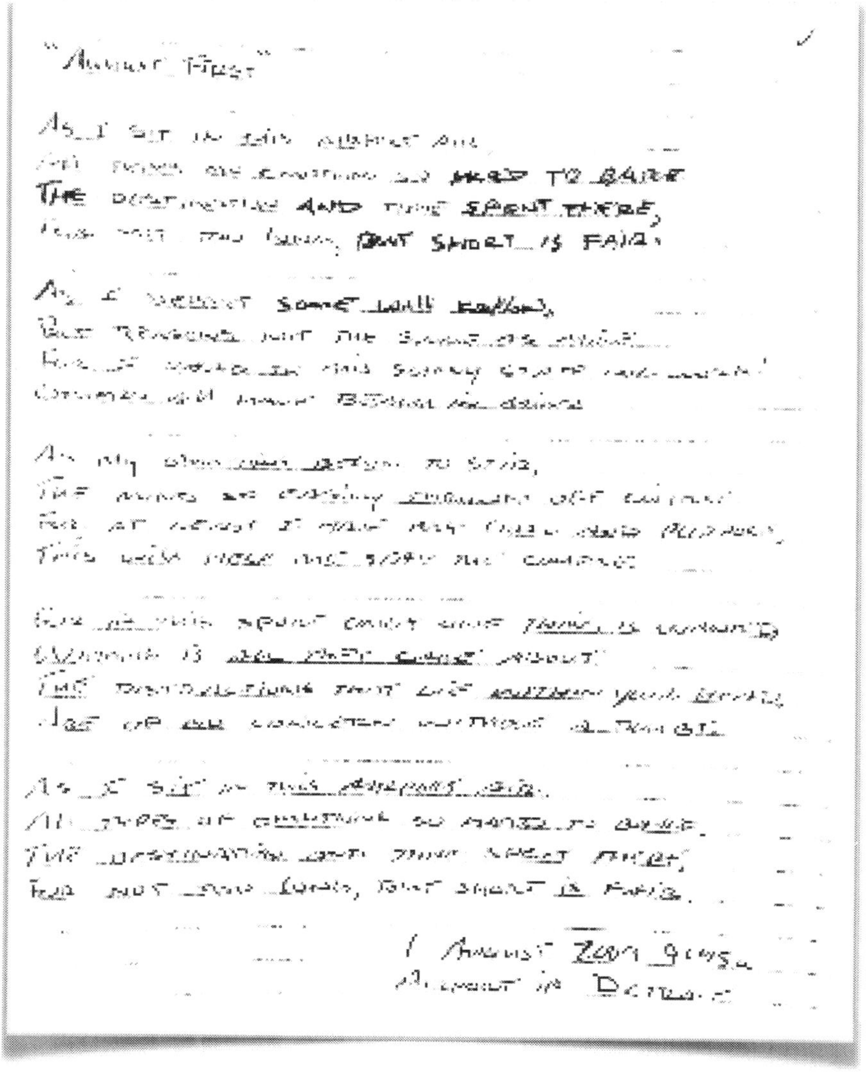

"August First"

As I sit in this [illegible]
[illegible] so hard to bare
The [illegible] and time spent there,
[illegible] but short is fair.

[illegible]

[illegible]

[illegible]

[illegible] but short is fair.

[illegible] August [illegible]

23. A World of Arrogance

Date: August 10, 2009
Time: 2:20 PM
Location: Clearwater, FL

"A World of Arrogance"

How far will these feelings take,
The person that may act above all others.
Uncertain as to why those feelings so strong,
This hostility can only go on for so long.

For first time this is not and you've been there before,
The actions the same and furthermore,
The banter continues for reasons unknown,
But faith in your heart is all that you know.

This type of person so bitter they are,
Comfort within themselves must be so far.
Even with all the confidence they hold,
This type of person they are far too cold.

Too continue to carry a conversation so empty,
Would be forced and frowned upon.
For the best thing to do in those situations,
Is to turn around and continue walk on.

Let those who will act this way do what they do,
For changing those people is not up to you.
Stay true to your self for friends they are not,
Sometimes yourself is all that you got.

Synopsis

During this time I was having a hard time with another player on my team. The unfortunate thing I had to deal with was the fact that I had to see this person every day and for some unknown reason he and I did not get along. The interesting thing in baseball is that there are egos larger than elephants all piled into one minor league/ major league locker room and there is no way everyone will get along.

"To continue to carry a conversation so empty…" Here I am referring to the fact that we, as humans, are only given so much time on this earth. Why spend our time here unhappy - talking with people we don't get along with when we can better enjoy our time talking with our friends? Don't waste your words with empty conversation. Rather, "Stay true to yourself…" and talk and interact with those you enjoy.

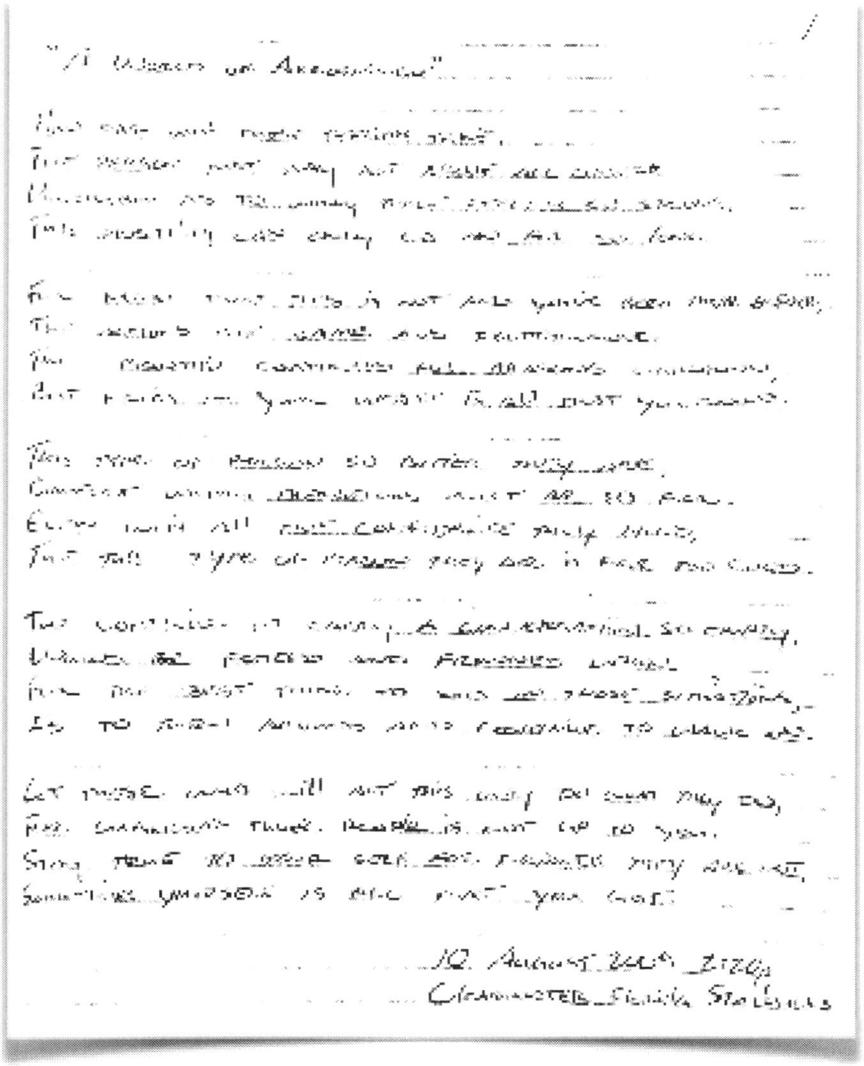

24. Same Sounds, New Waters

Date: August 10, 2009
Time: 2:00 PM
Location: Daytona Beach, Florida

"Same Sounds, New Waters"

As I lie under this moonlit night,
I hear the ocean waves crash to the shore.
Without any specific formation,
Carelessly breaking ever more.

All lengths and heights these waves come to shore,
The water rushing, the sound heard before.
Not at these beaches, but similar they are,
For the Pacific's impression an enjoyable scar.

On the memory of a child it is so strong,
Until the next wave comes crashing on in.
From listening to waves as one lies there in bed,
Each new wave carries the memory along.

Time stands still and thoughts do run wild,
Yet the ocean sounds keep peace in ones' heart.
The subtle breeze and the waves in the background,
Makes all this too hard when time comes to part.

Synopsis

Here is a piece I put together one late night after having one of the better outings in my baseball career. The condo I had at the time was on the 11th floor of this building that sat on the beach. As I lay there in bed with the window open, I could hear the waves crashing to the shore, waves that brought back memories of walking the Oregon coast beaches as a child. I am not sure how you feel, but being close to water just resonates well with me and keeps me calm and at ease. These feelings were imperative during my baseball careers as there were many ups and downs.

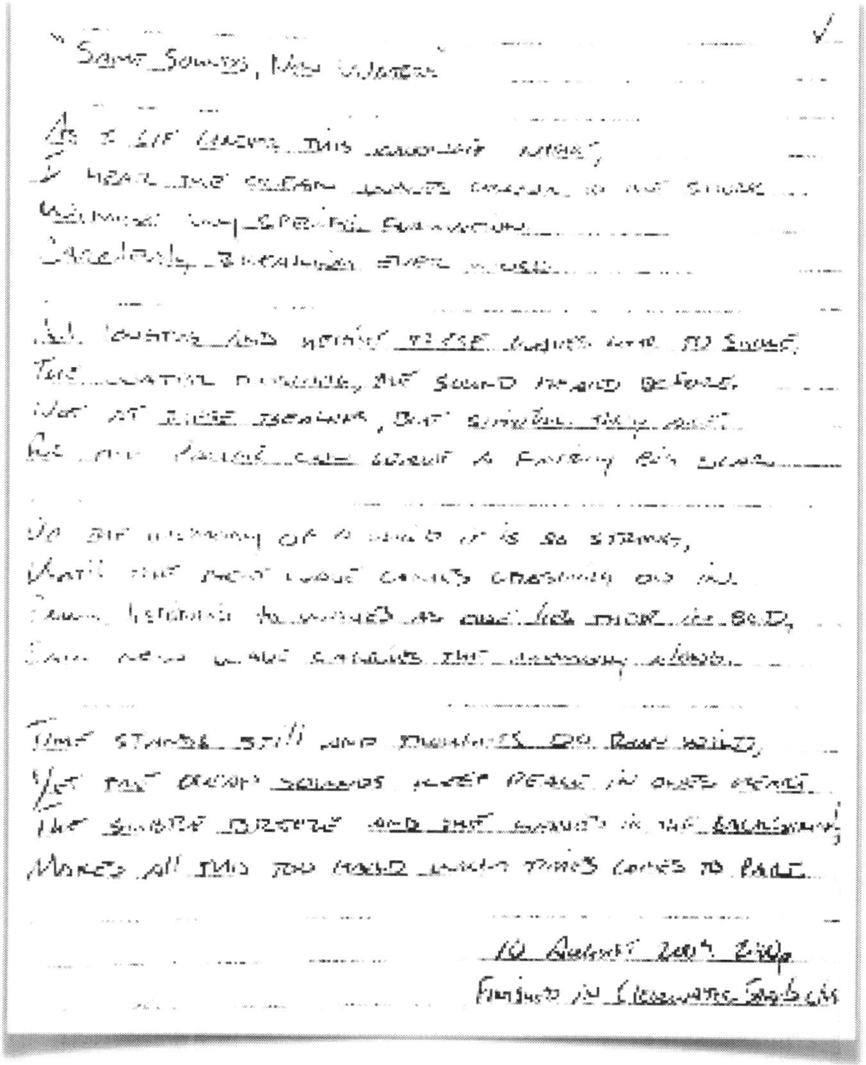
"Same Sounds, New Waters"

[illegible]

25. Day To Day

Date: August 18, 2009
Time: 1:00 AM
Location: Daytona Beach, Florida

"Day to Day"

The life is rough, room filled with arrogance,
But all have dreams and wish some way.
Dreams be meant and life be easy,
But each train less from day to day.

Put in time and work done right,
All would rather drink and play.
For nothing comes with ease in life,
Each train less from day to day.

All the talent in the world,
Can be dismissed without delay.
Taken for granted what some have,
Many train less from day to day.

Their time is ending the light in sight,
Yes all would rather finish today.
Throw out all hard work for temptation,
Last day has come to train this way.

Inspired by Desiderata "Quietly I go my way"

Synopsis

The athletes in professional sports who take for granted their God-given talents and rely on their abilities inspired this piece. For most, they fizzle out because when they get to the professional level, everyone shares their talents. The second stanza refers to the fact that many would rather party then train day in and day out because they think they are "good enough" to get the job done. Unfortunately, "Their time is ending the light in sight…" and they look back and can only say "what if."
Don't ever look back on opportunities you are given and say "if I only would have" or "what if." Attack each day as a new and make sure that at the end of each day you can look yourself in the mirror and be proud of your accomplishments and know you did everything you could to improve your life or someone else's life.

I also recommend "googling" Desiderata.

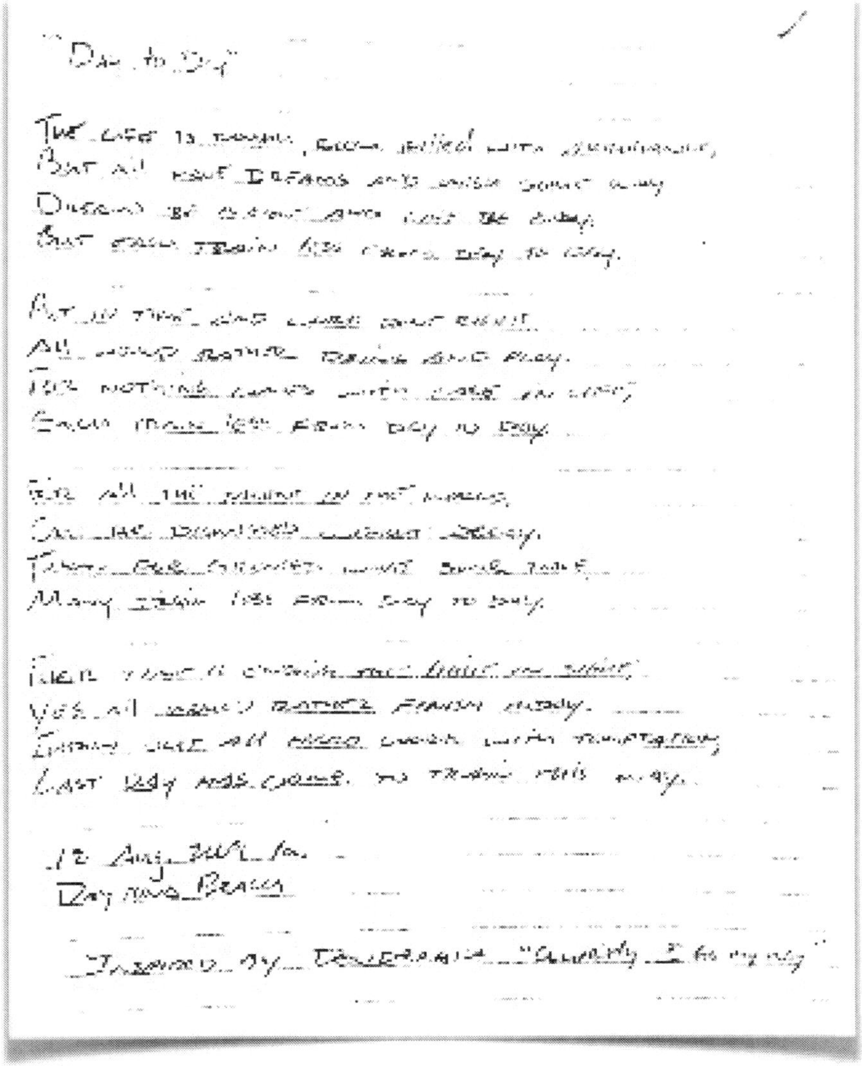

"Day to Day"

26. Appreciation

Date: November 9, 2009
Time: 1:35 AM
Location: Portland, Oregon

"Appreciation"

The appreciation for you is such,
Everything you have given, so much!
Affect everything I do,
My love for you,
Is eternal and amounts to much.

Each day a new upon rising,
And it is you to turn to for guidance!
Conversation can build,
Parties unhappy not thrilled,
But love from you is guiding.

The work you put in is hard,
But rewarding for each, do your part.
One day will come,
Where all is done,
You'll sit back content at heart.

So this I write for you,
My love for each is true.
Thank you both so much,

My life you have touched,
I owe it all to you.

Synopsis

This piece is about my parents, for my parents. I would not be who I am or as strong as I am today without my parents and the support they have given me throughout the years. I have endured a lot, not that others haven't. From injuries in baseball, to heart breaks to releases to graduations, my parents have been there the entire time. This is piece I wrote to thank them for everything they have done for me and to let them know that "My life you have touched, I owe it all to you."

Be thankful for your support systems, whoever or whatever they may be.

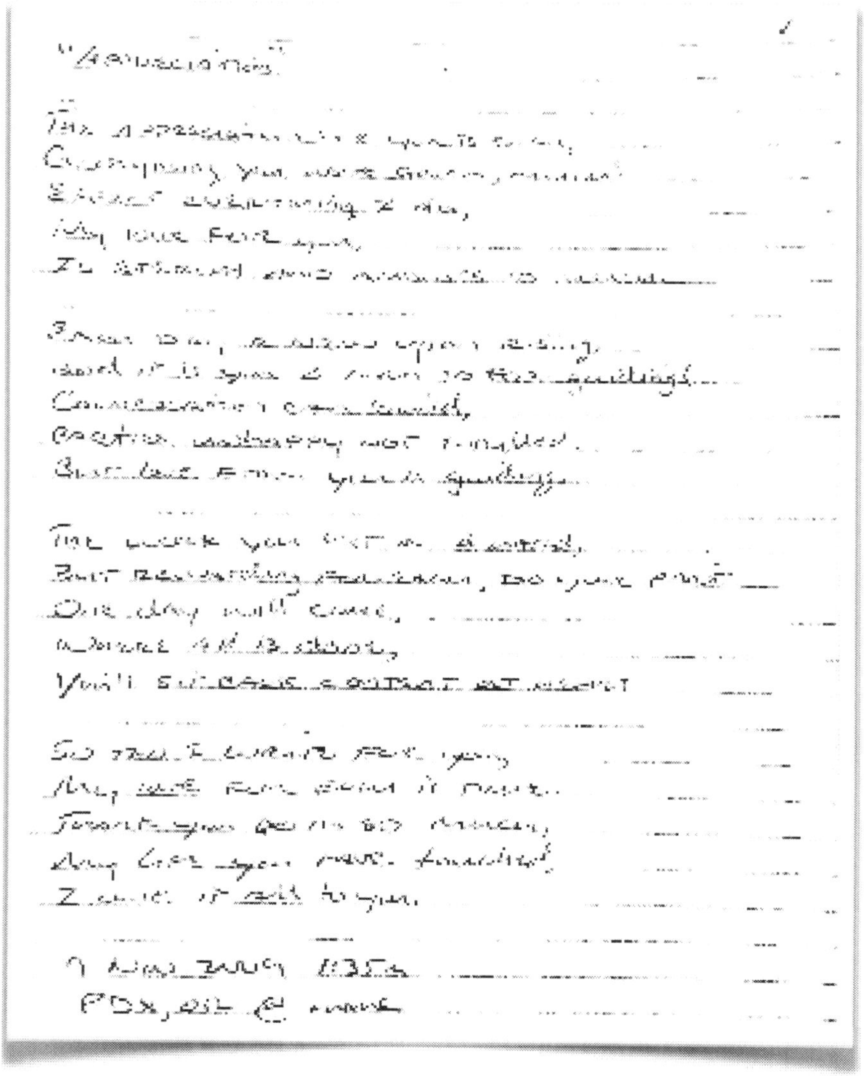
One day will come,

Hearts

27. Hesitation, No More

Date: March 24, 2013
Time: 2:00 AM
Location: Los Angeles, California

"Hesitation, No More"

At first you aren't sure what to think,
Losing track of those back home…not in mind.
Coming into a situation, the unknown,
A skeptic in present time.

I step out of that limo,
You…standing there beautiful in that dress.
I lost my breath for that moment,
Then thought, getting down on one knee would be best!

Time did go by,
The thought of you was all I had.
Until you gave me that chance,
On the dodge ball field…I wasn't all that bad.

Then it all clicked for me,
I knew on the top of that hotel, right then and there,
My feelings for you were building and real,
The skeptic in me to be found, nowhere!

We're dancing, we're talking, I'm thinking about us,

The possibility of you and I no longer an imagination for me.
But kissing you and holding you and sharing my life with you…
A must!

So as you go through this journey,
Along emotional roads not straight, but curvy.
Remember I'm here and I'm thinking of you,
And the thought of us now is ever so true!

Synopsis

There is a lot of information written in this piece. At first I didn't know how to react or respond to some of the situations I faced in the house and with her, but I knew that I was open to anything. I've had some pretty crazy experiences in life: sleeping on the floor of buses traveling to and from cities in the Midwest that no one has ever heard of, flying to Europe on a whim because I thought it would be a good idea, chasing a dream in that of baseball that would ultimately lead to a torn ligament in my elbow, relationships that I thought were strong but were only stepping stones to where I am today, etc.

This poem is a mixture of playfulness, "On the dodge ball field…I wasn't all that bad," to emotional certainty "The possibility of you and I no longer an imagination for me. But kissing you and holding you and sharing my life with you…A must."

I knew right after that dodge ball game that there was a chance that she could be the one for me. Those feelings solidified in our emotional dance together we shared that night.

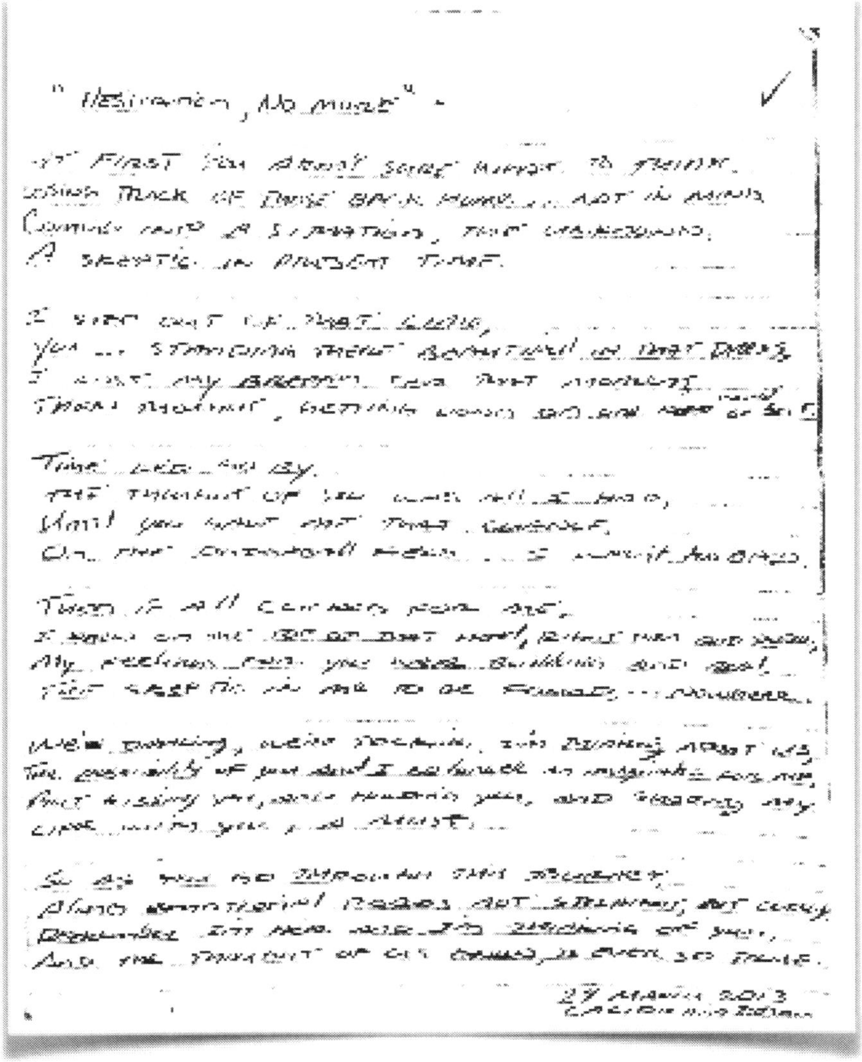

28. Revised Editions

Date: March 25, 2013
Time: 10:15 AM
Location: Plane to Atlantic City

"Revised Editions"

Let's go to a place you won't know,
See all of the film,
Cut for the show.

Tensions may rise,
But some of the guys
Will sit back and relax as it goes.

There are few involved with the chatter,
But back home the chatter is what matters.

To sell a good show,
Drama must flow,
For the girl and the rose is what matters.

Synopsis

Here is an interesting piece I wrote that I am going to leave to the reader to interpret and find the meaning behind the title, one of which is my favorite.

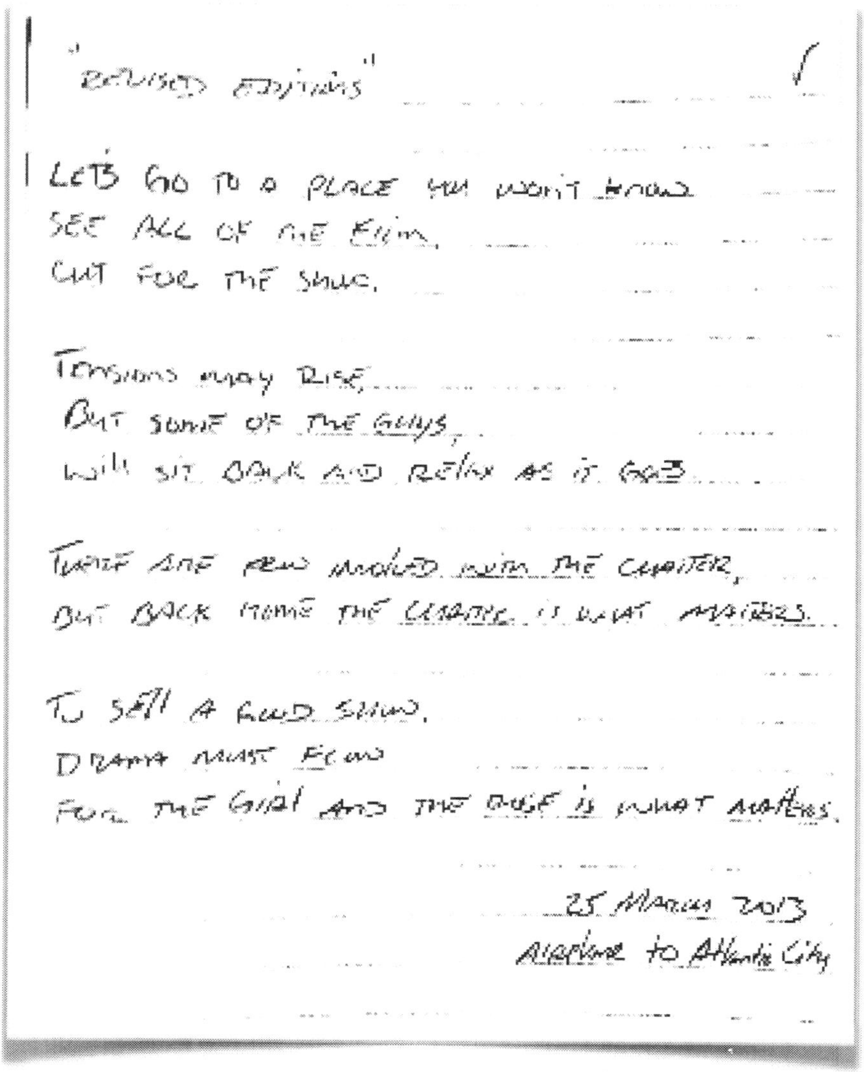

"REVISED EDITIONS"

LET'S GO TO A PLACE YOU WON'T KNOW
SEE ALL OF THE FILM,
CUT FOR THE SHOW.

TENSIONS MAY RISE,
BUT SOME OF THE GUYS,
WILL SIT BACK AND RELAX AS IT GOES.

THERE ARE FEW MOVED WITH THE CHAPTER,
BUT BACK HOME THE CHARACTER IS WHAT MATTERS.

TO SELL A GOOD SHOW,
DRAMA MUST FLOW
FOR THE GIRL AND THE ROSE IS WHAT MATTERS.

25 MARCH 2013
Airplane to Atlantic City

29. The Last and The First

Date: March 25, 2013
Time: 1:05 PM
Location: Airplane To Atlantic City

"The Last and The First"

Follow me as this flows,
For this may paint the most vivid picture.
Not with colors but with words,
Ink to paper here we go.

The plane just landed.
You have three black bags, luggage.
Your walk is swift, left-right-left-right.
Now all control is abandoned.

You have arrived into the unknown, a hotel room.
No phone, no computer, no work.
All you have are your thoughts,
But you are 100% alone.

The phone rings loud like a police siren just turned on as it zooms by you at the light,
Unsure of who the voice is, but you cooperate accordingly.
For ultimately this unknown experience is yours,
But do not resist the process, do not fight.

You prep with some pictures and dress to impress.
You are new to the interviews.
You are asked questions about love and feelings and emotions.
All of this to see if you can stand the test.

Then there in the back of your mind you hear a skeptic,
"What are you doing here?"
"Was this the right decision?"
Just roll with it although it's hectic.

See the skeptic confused with lack of control,
For all that he knows is a schedule.
Now forced to adhere to a plan he not knows,
The journey goes on and he follows.

Pull on to day four dressed tailored and fitted,
Short arm on seven long arm on nine.
Downstairs your black limo with champagne awaits you.
Take a deep breath, your committed.

Pull up to the house with a girl there to greet you,
You are ready and know what to say.
All the pacing in your room now finally over,
The last and the first the same day!

Synopsis

This is just a quick description of one of the most interesting experiences in my life that I am very thankful I experienced.

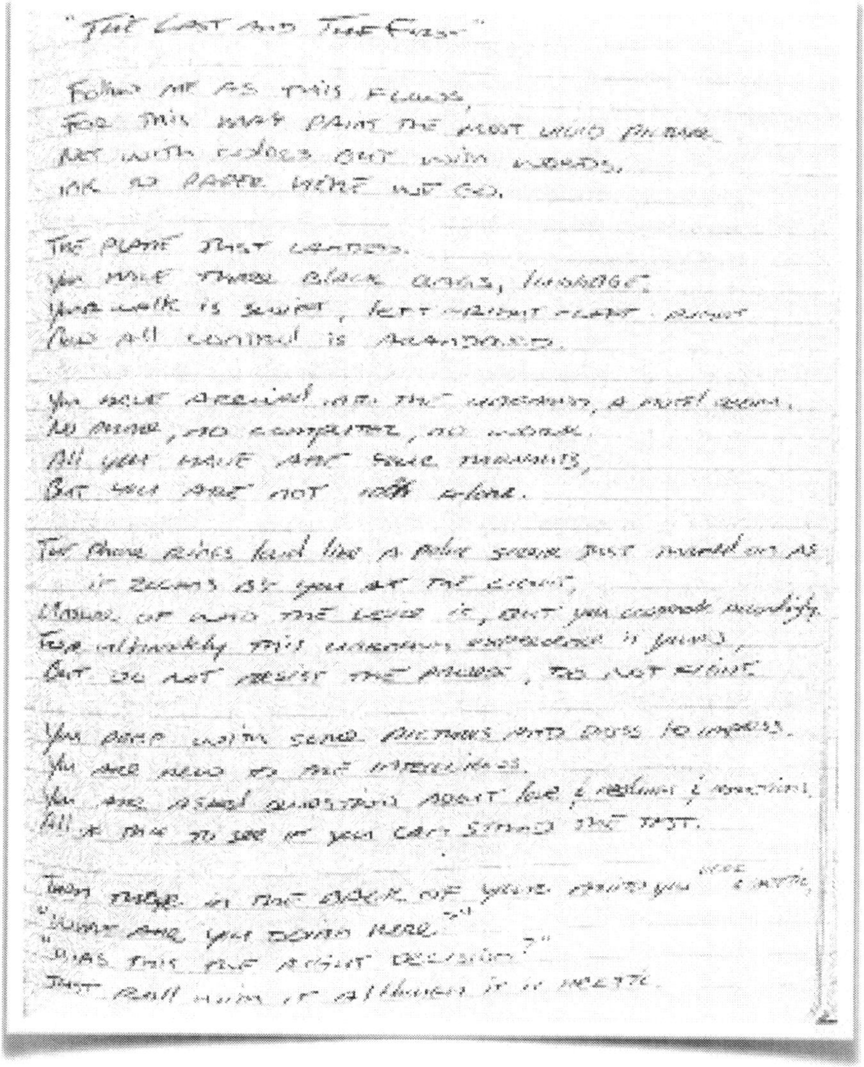

"The Last and The First"

Follow me as this flows,
For this may paint the most vivid picture
Not with colors but with words.
Ink to paper here we go.

The plane just landed.
You have three black bags, luggage.
Your walk is swift, left-right-left-right
And all control is abandoned.

You have arrived at the [illegible], a hotel room.
No phone, no computer, no work.
All you have are your thoughts,
But you are not [illegible] alone.

The phone rings loud like a fire alarm just [illegible] as
it zooms by you at the [illegible],
Unsure of who the [illegible] is, but you [illegible] [illegible].
[illegible] this [illegible] experience is [illegible],
But do not resist the [illegible], do not fight.

You [illegible] with [illegible] [illegible] and [illegible] to impress.
You are [illegible] to the [illegible].
You are asked questions about love & feelings & emotions,
All a [illegible] to see if you can stand the test.

[illegible] [illegible] in the back of your mind you [illegible] [illegible],
"What are you doing here?"
"Was this the right decision?"
Just roll with it although it is [illegible].

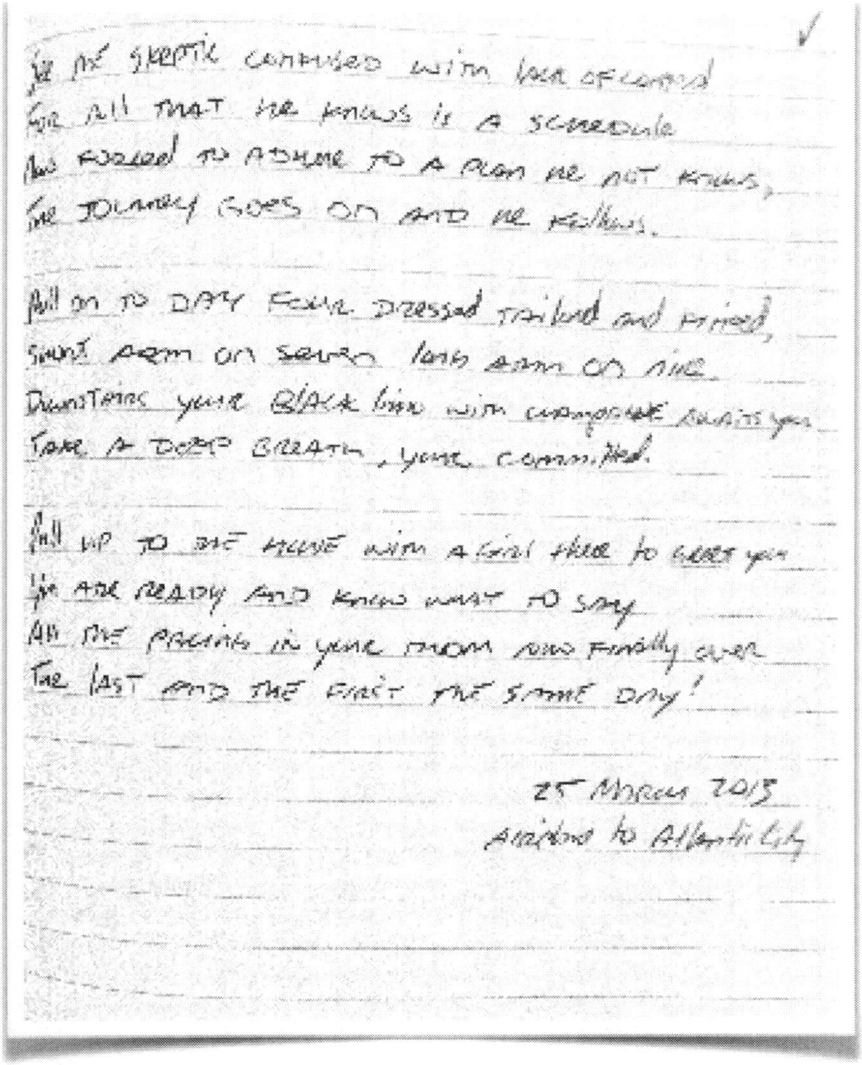

He the skeptic confused with lack of control
For all that he knows is a schedule
And forced to adhere to a plan he not knows,
The journey goes on and he follows.

Pull on to day four dressed tailored and primed,
Short arm on seven long arm on nine
Downstairs your black limo with champagne awaits you
Take a deep breath, your committed.

Pull up to the house with a girl there to greet you
You are ready and know what to say
All the pacing in your room now finally over
The last and the first the same day!

25 March 2015
Arizona to Atlantic City

30. Thoughts So True

Date: April 1, 2013
Time: 4:00 AM
Location: Munich, Germany

"Thoughts So True"

While I stand there waiting watching you,
You're dressed so perfect, you look so cute.
You reach for red a chance you'll take,
But choice is right and your mind is made.

While I stand there waiting watching you,
My mind at ease my eyes are glued.
All I can think of is you and me,
One choice is me, this gets more true.

While I stand there waiting my thoughts run free,
Thoughts of past relationships…old to me.
Girls I used to think were true,
All out of mind as I think of you.

While I stand there waiting my feelings grow,
New thoughts of you are all I know.
The plan here now not up to me,
Feelings eternal if you choose me.

Synopsis

Here is a general idea of my feelings during rose ceremonies. Every single time I had the opportunity to stand there in front of Des, I couldn't help but notice how beautiful she was.

Stanza II - my mind was truly at ease because I had the confidence in our relationship that we were meant to be together. I felt that every time we were around each other - our actions and conversation felt natural.

Stanza III and IV- My thoughts literally were not of past relationships, but only of her and I was truly happy those past experiences brought me to this point. While all I could do was hope that she was feeling the same way, I knew in my heart what I wanted. Feelings eternal if she chose me.

"Thoughts So True".

While I stand there waiting watching you,
You're dressed so perfect, you look so cute.
You reach for [illegible] a choice you'll [illegible].
But choice is right and your mind is made.

While I stand there waiting watching you,
My mind at ease my eyes are closed
All I can think of is me and you,
One choice is me, this gets more true.

While I stand there waiting my thoughts [illegible] free
Thoughts of past relationships ... old to me.
Girls I used to think were true,
All out of mind as I think of you.

While I stand there waiting my feelings flowing
New thoughts of you are all I know.
The plan were made [illegible] up to me
Feelings eternal if you choose me.

1 April 2013
Heading to Munich
@ 41[illegible]

31. Concealed Truth

Date: April 3, 2013
Time: 2:45 AM
Location: Munich, Germany

"Concealed Truth"

Well stories unfold not true,
But opposite of what you expect them to do.
You are here for the right reasons,
Experience is new,
But jaded you may be once the journey is through.

Unless all was revealed in an instance.
New decisions for you may be hard.
Perspective you'll keep,
But wrong thought this might be,
The process, the downfall and existence.

Keep in mind some feelings are real,
Expressed by those who are ready and feel.
You can be the one,
Easy decision is none,
Don't be blinded by the ones who conceal.

Synopsis

Here we have one of my poems that I felt compelled to write at 2:30 in the morning because I could not sleep. The last line in stanza one speaks to the possibility that, while I was on the show for the right reasons, others may have not been and it was potentially going to leave a sour taste in my mouth after the journey was all said and done.

Stanza two speaks directly to Des. When drama broke out between some of the guys, I was worried that it may be overwhelming for her. The reason I use the words "Perspective you'll keep, but wrong thought this might be," is because I was afraid she may not see the true side of some people in the house, or at least the side that we saw. Line five I will leave up to you to analyze. Let's just say it is thought provoking…

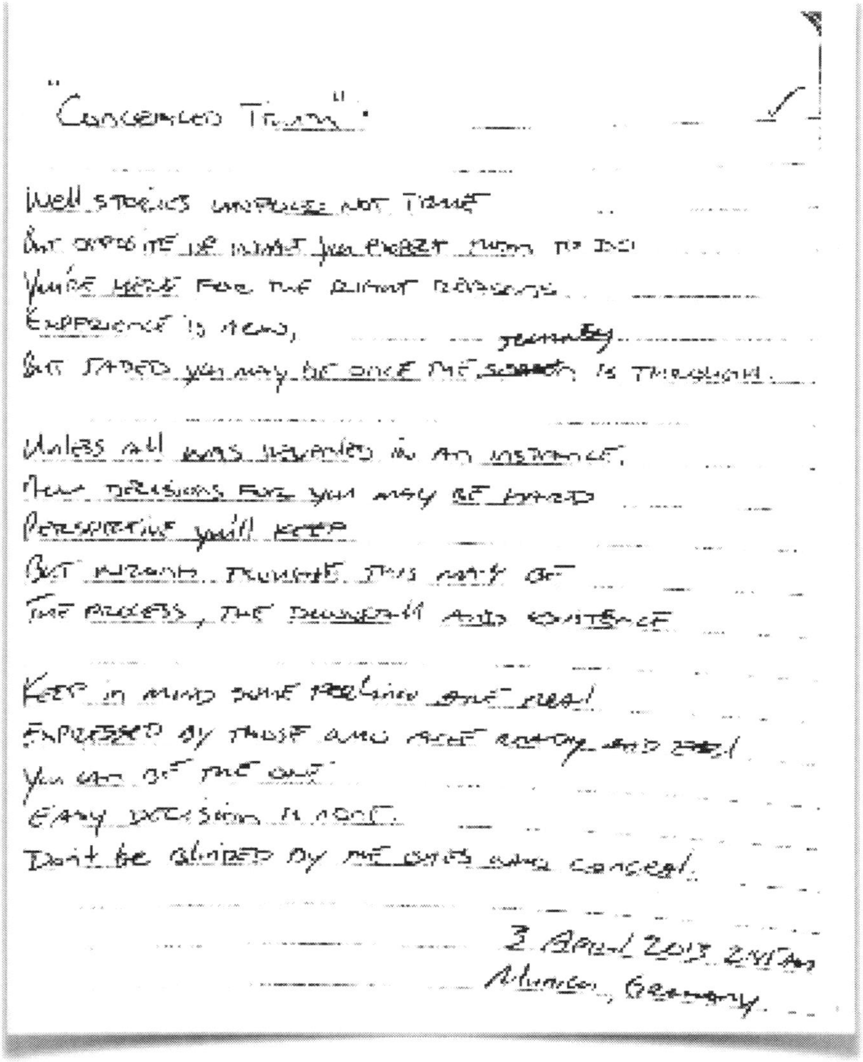

"Concealed Truth":

Well stories unfold not true
But opposite of what you expect them to do
You're here for the right reasons
Experience is new, journey
But faded you may be once the search is through.

Unless all was revealed in an instance,
Then decisions for you may be based
Perspective you'll keep
But wisdom, triumph, this may get
The process, the strength and existence

Keep in mind some feelings are real
Expressed by those who are ready and real
You are of the one
Every decision is good.
Don't be blinded by the ones who conceal.

3 April 2013 2:41am
Munich, Germany.

32. Closely Listening

Date: April 5, 2013
Time: 7:30 AM
Location: Barcelona, Spain

"Closely Listening"

Do we deserve to judge others for things they do?
For decisions they've chosen haven't yet affected you.
But now in this moment decisions they've made,
Affect not just you but the one they persuade.

Two faces turn one and unfold stories not true,
For lies that are told are more frustrations for you.
But why does this man hide behind the words that he says?
For truth will be told and spoils be made.

Unfortunate this may be for blinded is she,
By the words and feelings she holds so close to her heart.
But jaded she'll be and stronger woman we'll know,
For this part only a piece of her heart.

So may truth be told and let true feelings prevail,
This journey unique in a way.
And never remember the ones that weren't honest,
For now your time will be far apart!

Synopsis

As you can see I wrote this poem during a very intense time on the show when there was a little more drama than I was accustomed to. The main point here and is that in life it is important to not put on a façade when you are meeting people or working on building relationships, whether it be friendships, work relationships, etc. because the real you will ultimately be revealed by yourself or exposed by others. In the third stanza I am speaking about Des and what we presume she does and does not know. She's gone through some tough decisions and the last thing I personally wanted during this time, at this point in the process was for her to be jaded and to think none of us were there for the right reasons.

"Cloudy Listening"

Do we deserve to judge others for things they do?
For decisions they've chosen haven't yet affected you.
But now in this moment decisions they've made,
Affect not just you but the one they persuade.

Two faces turn one and unfold stories not true,
For lies that are told are more frustrations for you.
But why does this man hide behind the words that he says?
For truth will be told and spoils be made.

Unfortunate this may be for blinded is she,
By the words and feelings she holds so close to her heart.
But jaded she'll be and stronger woman we'll know
For this part only a piece of her heart

So may truth be told and let true feelings prevail,
This journey unique in a way.
And never remember the ones that weren't honest,
For now your time will be far apart!

5 April 2013
Plane to Barcelona
@ 7:30am

33. Day Dreaming

Date: April 11, 2013
Time: 2:00 PM
Location: Plane To Portugal

"Day Dreaming"

As I sit in this car I reflect on what happened,
The longest weekend to date.
Drama ran rampant and tension so thick!
But we found you could not be persuaded.

Voices around me talk in excitement,
But for me all I do is daydream.
About you and I and the fun we are having,
Excited about what we could be!

As I sit in this car I can't help but wonder,
How our first walk side by side will go.
No cameras around and your hand in mine,
Off to breakfast we'll go!

Voices around me discuss the past,
And all I can see is your face.
The image so clear as if you are right here,
How my mind longs for that day.

As I sit in this car my mind free of worry,
For I know you are the one for me.

Back to the present still future in mind,
And in time I'll get down on one knee!

Synopsis

Here I am coming off of an emotional high with Des. She just expressed to me her feelings through poetry and I was ecstatic! The second stanza speaks to the fact that all of the guys with me at the time were excited to go out and explore the city, but the only thing I could do was daydream about the thought of her and I together forever. Sometimes you don't need to entertain the one you are with or the one you want to be with. Sometimes all you want to do is share a cup of coffee together or sit together over breakfast and people watch.

That is the way I feel with Des. I don't need to entertain her and if we don't have anything to say to each other, it is OK! because we enjoy each other's company so much.

The last stanza really emphasizes my confidence in my journey to find love and a lasting relationship with Des. I was not worried about anything because I knew in my heart she was the one for me and no matter what would happen, we would ultimately be together. I Just Had A Feeling that is hard to describe.

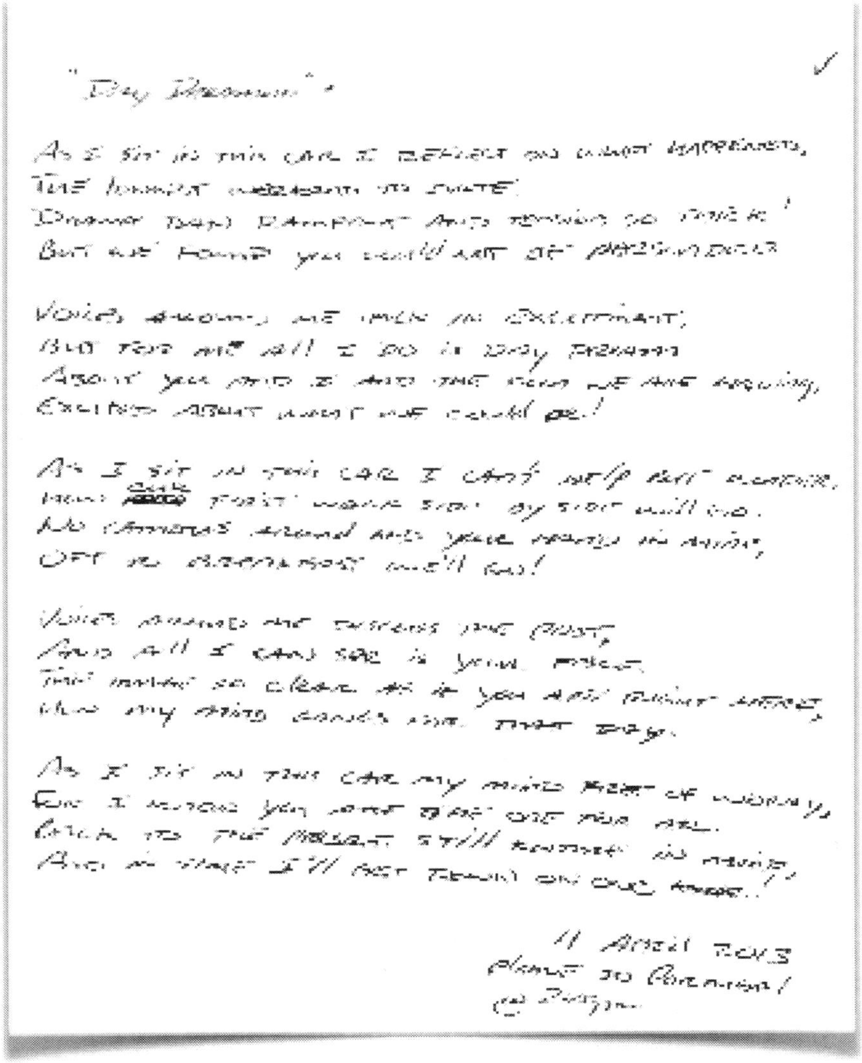

"Day Dream" *

As I sit in this car I reflect on what happened,
The longest weekend to date!
Dinner then [illegible] and [illegible] so [illegible]!
But we found you couldn't get [illegible]

Voices around me full of excitement;
But for me all I do is day dream
About you and I and the life we are building,
Excited about what we could be!

As I sit in this car I can't help but wonder,
How [illegible] those first [illegible] by first will go.
No cameras around and your hands in mine,
Off on [illegible] we'll go!

Voices around me [illegible] the past,
And all I can see is your face,
That image so clear as if you were right there,
When my [illegible] [illegible] that day.

As I sit in this car my mind [illegible] of worry,
For I know you [illegible] once and for all.
Back to the present still [illegible] in [illegible],
And in time I'll get down on one knee!"

11 April 2013
[illegible] to [illegible] /
@ [illegible]

34. Smile

Date: April 11, 2013
Time: 2:30 PM
Location: Plane To Portugal

"Smile"

You Smile,
I look,
You notice,
It's great!

I smile,
You look,
Connection,
We've made!

I know it is real,
Connection I feel,
Comes only but once in a while!

For you with me,
Is all I can see,
Please smile at me for a while!

Synopsis

This was something I put together very quick. The first stanza speaks to our time on the dodge ball field and every group date I was on. Her and I had a connection that was far different than everyone else. She could be across the room and look over and see me – we'd make eye contact and smile at one another – and we knew both of us were ok and did not need to be entertaining one another. It is a rare feeling but for her to validate those feelings by expressing the same thing to me, this connection I felt, meant the world to me and allowed me to completely be open to her and the experience we were sharing together.

"Smile" . /68

You Smile,
I look,
You notice,
It's great!

I smile,
You look,
Connection!
We've made!

I know it is real,
connection I feel,
comes only but once in a while!

For you with me,
is all I can see,
Please smile at me for a while!

11 April 2013
Plane to Portugal!
@ 2:30pm

35. Individually Defined

Date: April 14, 2013
Time: 1:10 AM
Location: Madeira, Portugal

"Individually Defined"

The strongest word with so much meaning,
Hard to say without a stammer.
But when expressed with true feelings,
Sincere, for no other word can mean so much more.

Like the time we had,
Atop the hotel seventeen above.
Feelings had changed and were oh so real,
Meant to be, is how I feel.

"Our hearts are open" words expressed by you,
Feelings that I know are so true.
"I look forward to the unknown and appreciate your
emotions you have shown,"
And I am also hopeful to see if in your heart
I have found a home.

Vivid are the memories of,
Each moment I spent with you.
Subtle hints we share together,
Keep me falling forward each day of new.

Expressed in writing and felt through touch,
Embrace these qualities that define this word:
Faith, Hope, Charity, Kindness, Patience, Sympathy,
Forgiveness, Unselfishness, Courage.
Knowing THESE and THIS can last forever,
Enjoy this moment, embrace this rush.

The strongest word with so much meaning,
Not so hard to believe it's true.
"Our hearts are open and in every kiss,"
I truly mean: **I LOVE YOU!**

Synopsis

This may be the most emotional piece I've ever written. I capitalized the beginning of the middle four stanzas to show you how I accidentally spelled the word love in a poem that I wrote to her to confess my feelings of love for her. It was as if it was meant to be. Love is not a word I use loosely. In fact, I have only said it twice in past relationships. I am not sure if you could tell I was nervous, but I WAS! The quotes in stanza three and six are in reference to a piece of poetry she shared with me that meant so much. I felt it was only necessary to include them in my most emotional poem to her.

Along the way we shared "subtle hints" or signs that we cared for each other throughout this journey and I think those were what gave me the confidence that her and I could work. It is important to note that I truly wanted to express to her what I thought the word Love meant and so I defined it to the best of my ability. I understand that love has many different meanings to each and every one of us and my definitions of the word love may not line up with yours, but I wanted to share with her about how I truly felt.

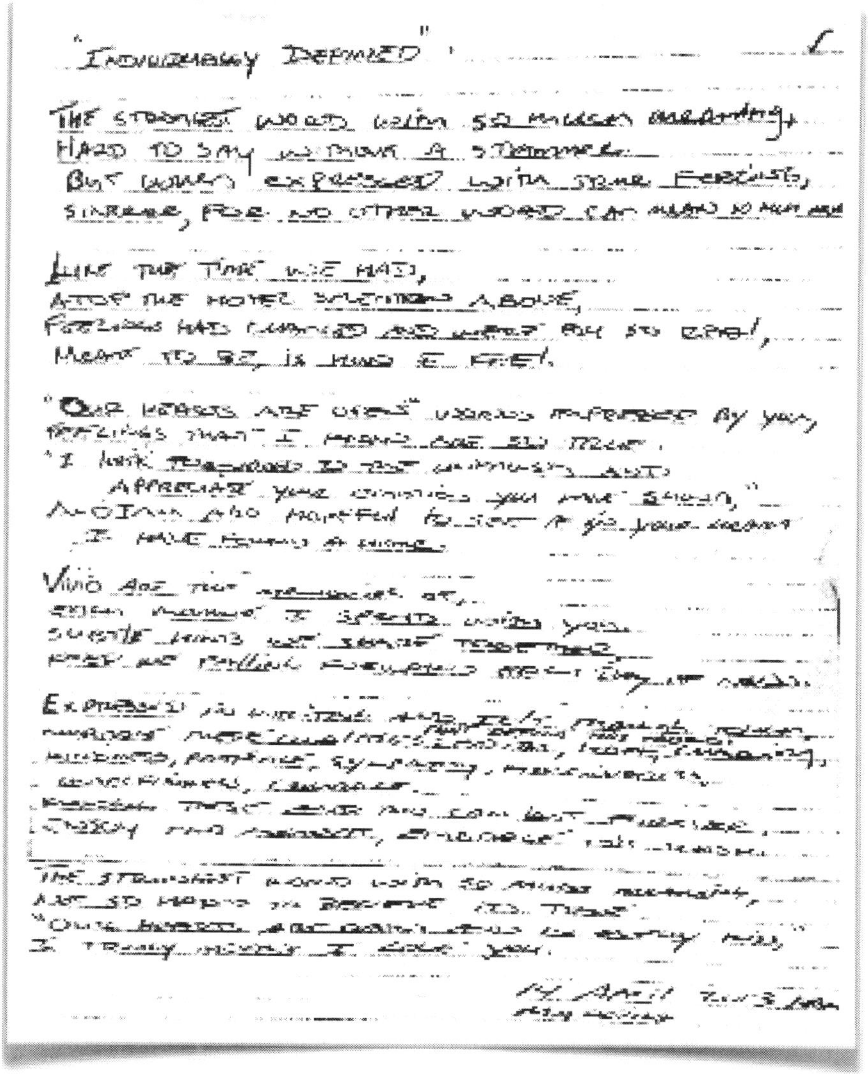

"INDIVIDUALLY DEFINED"

THE STRONGEST WORD WITH SO MUCH MEANING,
HARD TO SAY WITHOUT A STAMMER..
BUT WHEN EXPRESSED WITH TRUE FEELINGS,
SINCERE, FOR NO OTHER WORD CAN [illegible]

LIKE THE TIME WE HAD,
ATOP THE HOTEL [illegible] ABOVE,
FEELINGS HAD [illegible] AND [illegible] SO REAL,
MEANT TO BE, IS [illegible] I FEEL.

"OUR HEARTS ARE OPEN" WORDS [illegible] BY YOU,
FEELINGS THAT I [illegible] ARE SO TRUE.
"I HAVE [illegible] TO [illegible] AND
APPRECIATE THE [illegible] YOU HAVE SHOWN,"
[illegible] AND [illegible] YOUR HEART
I HAVE FOUND A HOME.

WHO ARE THE [illegible] OF,
EACH MOMENT I SPEND WITH YOU.
[illegible] WE SHARE TOGETHER
KEEP ME [illegible] FORWARD [illegible].

EXPRESSED [illegible]

[illegible]

THE STRONGEST WORD WITH SO MUCH MEANING,
AND SO HARD TO [illegible] ITS TRUE
"OUR HEARTS ARE OPEN [illegible]"
I TRULY [illegible] I LOVE YOU.

[illegible]

36. Memories of Old and New

Date: April 16, 2013
Time: 7:45 PM
Location: Lisbon to Newark

"Memories of Old and New"

How happy I am to see you here,
In my hometown where I spent my younger years.
All these memories I can now share with you,
And reminisce of memories we created that are so new.

Now new memories are built as we are hand in hand,
My love for you declared in far off lands.
And passion we share in every kiss,
Let's stay like this so I won't have to miss…

My favorite things that make you who you are:
Your drive, your eyes, your creativity, your humor.
The comfort I feel around you even when we don't talk,
It feels like we've been best friend forever.

Let's share this moment we have together,
I'm hopeful these feelings last forever.
For now let's enjoy this NW weather,
And share a kiss, just like the first, during that
dance we had together.

Synopsis

This was a quick piece I put together to share with her on my hometown date to let her know how I felt for her and where I stood. It is quirky and fun and that is exactly what I wanted my hometown date to feel like, quirky and fun.

At the same time I wanted her to meet my family and show her how serious I was about her. I think the first stanza gives you a great description of my feelings towards her and how natural our relationship was when we were together.

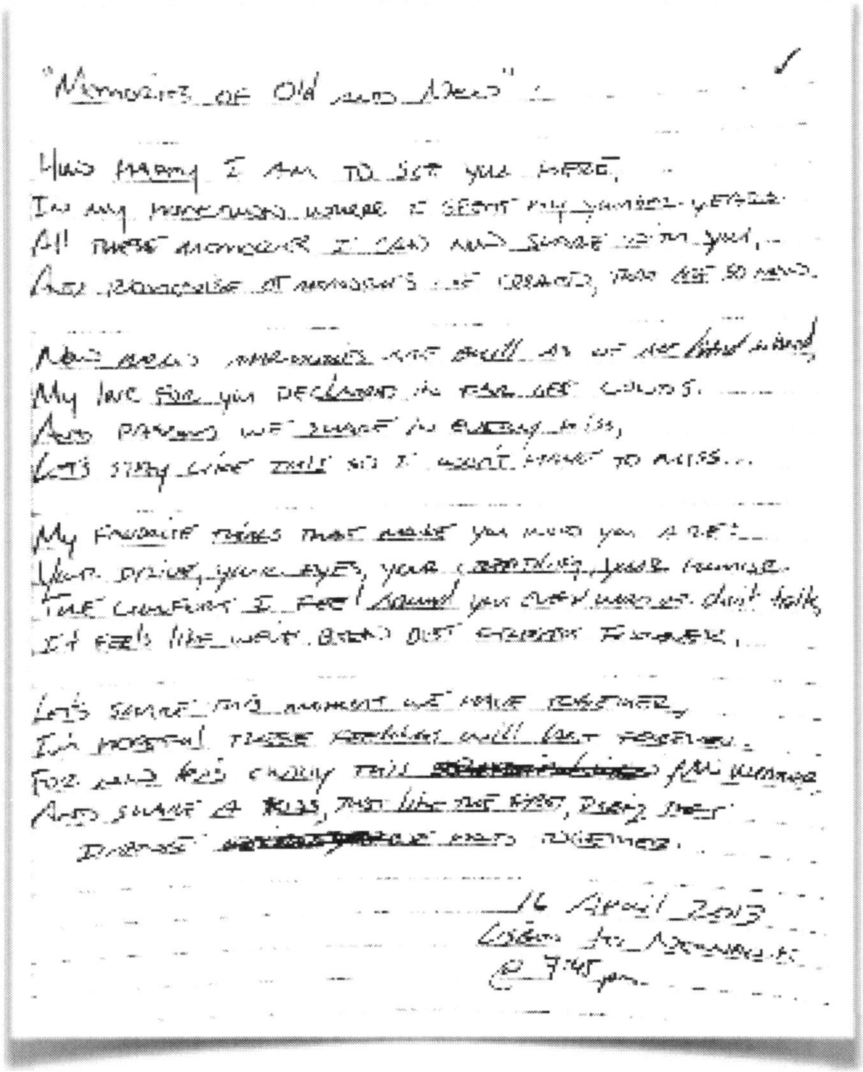

"Memories of Old and New"

How happy I am to see you here,
In my hometown where I spent my younger years.
All these memories I can and share with you,
And [illegible] of memories we created, they are so new.

New ones memories are [illegible] as we are hand in hand,
My love for you declared in [illegible] words.
And passion we share in every kiss,
Let's stay like this so I won't have to miss...

My favorite things that make you who you are...
Your smile, your eyes, your [illegible], your [illegible].
The comfort I feel around you even when we don't talk,
It feels like we've been best friends forever.

Let's savor this moment we have together,
I'm hopeful these feelings will last forever.
For and he's [illegible] till [illegible] all [illegible]
And share a kiss, just like the first, [illegible]
[illegible] [illegible] years together.

16 April 2013
[illegible]
@ 7:45 pm

37. Sitting, Waiting, Searching

Date: April 18, 2013
Time: 5:00 PM
Location: Los Angeles to Portland

"Sitting, Waiting, Searching"

You go through life searching for the one,
Hopeful to find her before your age grows the opposite of young.
And search you do from city to city,
But timing not right and the girl you look for a mystery.

"Don't be picky!"
Your friends do preach.
But who are they
To feel they can teach?

Position before.
They are so used to
These feelings you have
Are not so new.

Continue this journey and don't be discouraged,
For the girl for you is out there and is real.
Keep your eyes and mind not narrow but opened,

For the next one you find may be the one for you!

Synopsis

This poem is about patience in searching for love. I've dated girls in the past where I wanted to have true feelings and wanted there to be something, but pushing and hoping was ultimately not the best route to take. It is important to not jump into relationships because of loneliness. Everyone has a story to tell about a relationship, whether it be friendship or romantic, that didn't go as you thought it would or should. I decided to partake in this journey because I was open to the fact that it could work and there was no reason to not give it a chance. It was an experience I had never had so why not see if true love was out there and see if I could find a connection with Des.

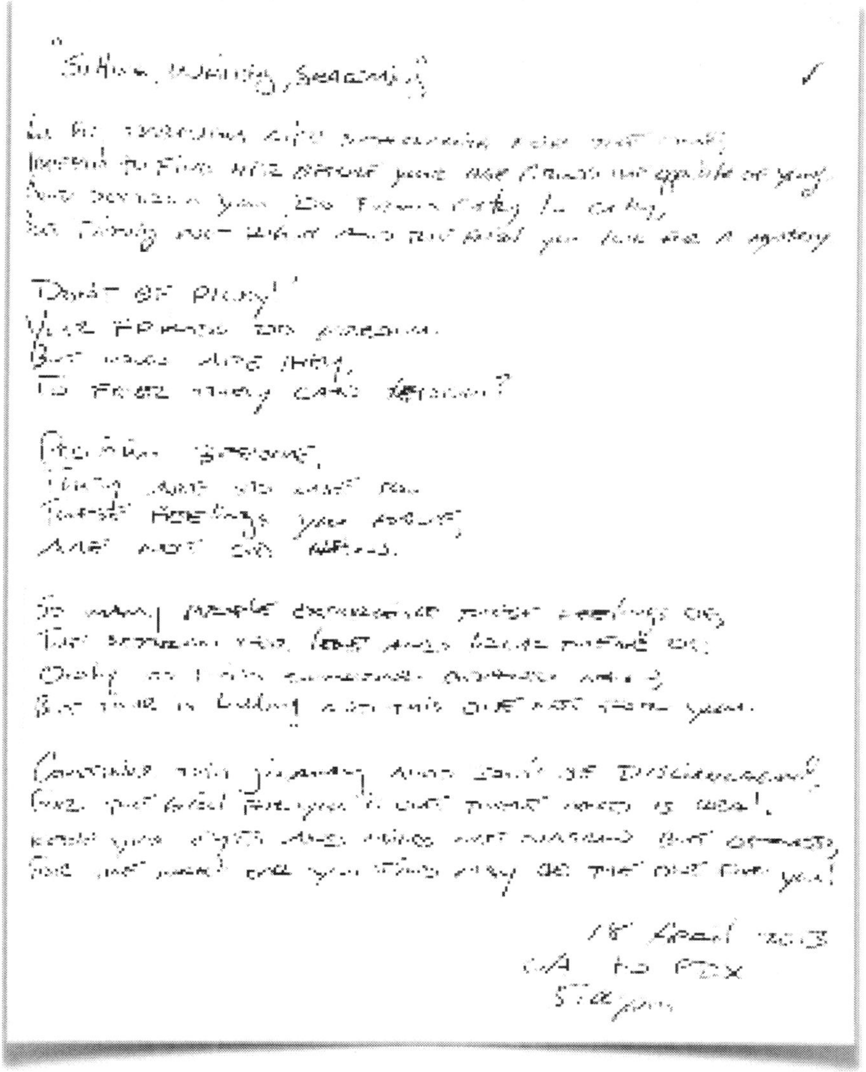

"Sitting, Waiting, Searching"

[illegible]

[illegible]

[illegible]

[illegible]

[illegible]

18th April 2013
CA to PDX
[illegible]

38. Distance in Mind

Date: April 27, 2013
Time: 11:30 PM
Location: LAX to JFK

"Distance in Mind"

I'm sitting here sleep interrupted,
For the thoughts that creep in mind are doubt.
All the moments we've shared together,
Potentially excused because of a quiet variable.

The variable of distance keeps me awake,
Something I want to ignore but is real.
Casually discussed to stay in the moment,
But looming in the depths of our minds.

To concede would bring doubt and uncertainty,
Not for the relationship we are building…
That of which I have full faith in,
But for the ability to provide for the future.

Both find comfort in the environment they reside in,
Compromise looks to be the only solution.
While not the same position,
Similar to before.

Worried history may repeat itself,

The guard slowly goes up and absence and time does pass.
But when brought together all previous, forgotten.
Stay in the moment and all will work out.

Synopsis

Besides being hot and miserable on my flight to Antigua, The flight to Antigua was emotional. Line four speaks to a "quiet variable," a variable of distance and moving for one another. The reason I use the word "quiet" is because while I did speak with Des occasionally about moving to Seattle, it was never a serious conversation. I knew I had a job that I wanted to keep and I knew that I would be able to support a family in the future, but it was imperative I did that in Seattle for the beginning of our long lasting relationship.

Stanza four speaks to relationships in the past where moving or breaking up was the only option and that was a lot of added pressure.

While I didn't completely close myself off in line two in the last stanza, I was nervous about having a serious conversation with Des about moving because I was afraid of losing her. The blessing was that every time I was with her and every time I am with her now all worries go away and I know in my heart she is the only one for me. I knew that if I were to just stay in the moment everything would work out and we would end up together.

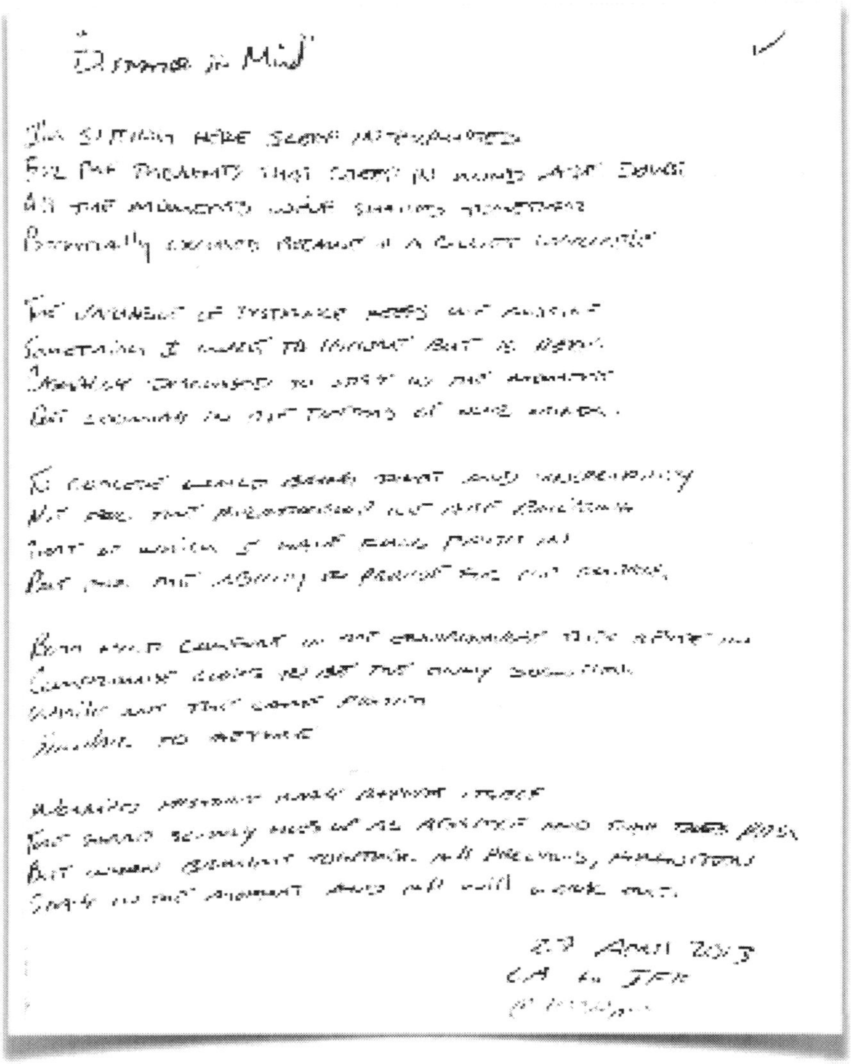

39. Forever a Part of the Plan

Date: April 27, 2013
Time: 11: 55 PM
Location: LAX to JFK

"Forever a Part of the Plan"

Exposed by the process of a new experience,
But one you believe in and one that may work.
For the connection you have hasn't been felt in a while,
Trust that the feelings are real and true.

Cast out the negativity that so easily clouds the mind,
For all that brings is doubt.
And remember the moments you've shared together,
Unforgettable memories that will last forever.

Only time will tell if it is meant to be,
Time so slow passing, feeling like eternity.
But time may play in ones favor,
Because with the absence of time the heart does grow
fonder.

Relax and remember this all a part of the process,
Keeping in mind the good feelings you share.
Have faith in what you are building,

For this is all a part of the plan.

Synopsis

This experience was none like I had ever experienced before and it really made me realize what I wanted in life and in a wife. I knew that if I stayed true to my feelings, I would be able to completely open up and show Des who I really was inside and what kind of man I really could be. It was important for me to never let negativity "cloud" my mind and I did a very good job at compartmentalizing all the friendships I had on the show. I knew that I was there to see if I could find love with Des and I would only dwell on the moments we shared together on our journey to find love, memories that will last forever. I am so thankful for the opportunity.

Time sometimes passed very slow for me, but it definitely played in my favor because I was able to really dig deep and find myself and make sure I wanted what my heart desired. "My heart does grow fonder" with the absence of time. In the thick of the situation it is sometimes hard to realize what you are building together, but I knew that if I had faith in our relationship and the overall plan, we would ultimately end up together!

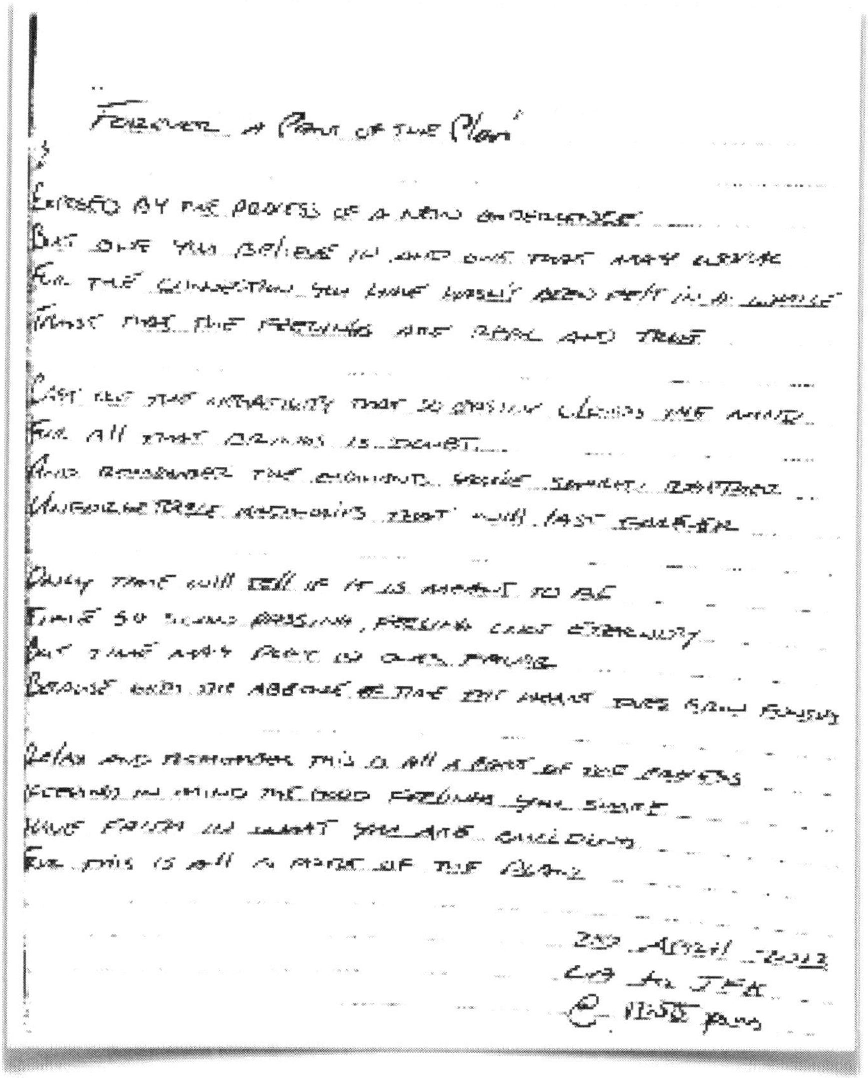

Forever a Part of the Plan

Excited by the process of a new [illegible]
But one you believe in and one that may [illegible]
For the connection you have hasn't been felt in a while
Trust that the feelings are real and true

Cast out the negativity that so easily clouds the mind
For all that brings is doubt...
And remember the moments you've shared together
Unforgettable moments that will last forever

Only time will tell if it is meant to be
Time so [illegible] passing, feeling like eternity
But time may [illegible]
Because [illegible]

Relax and remember this is all a part of the process
Keeping in mind the good feelings you share
Have faith in what you are building
For this is all a part of the plan

2nd April [illegible]
[illegible] JFK
C. [illegible]

40. Piecing Together Forever

Date: April 27, 2013
Time: 3:15 PM
Location: Antigua

"Piecing Together Forever"

It's exciting to see how far this journey has taken us,
From places I never knew existed,
To places I've longed to see.
All experiences you and I have shared together.

And now here we are,
One week after you met my family,
One week from the possibility of forever,
And I'm not nervous, I'm excited!

It's hard to deny the connection we've made.
True chemistry, real compatibility, permanent friendship,
All very important pieces to this puzzle of life;
And you and I fit well together.

So let's continue to fall forward,
Piecing together this journey with new memories.
Open to what is to come for us in the future
And excited to spend our lives together forever!

Synopsis

I really did enjoy this title. The idea here was that her and I would piece our lives together and it was not just "her" or "I" but "US" to me. I never once felt nervous about my feelings towards Des, even though I had no idea how organically the other relationships were growing. We had true chemistry that may sometimes have been missed through the lens, but I will never forget it.

Stanza IV - "So let's continue to fall forward" might be one of my favorite lines because it infers that while we are moving forward, there will be hiccups along the way, but that each obstacle we run into will only make us grow stronger every day.

"Piecing Together Forever" ✓

It's exciting to see how far this journey has taken us
From places I never knew existed
To places I've wanted to see
All experiences you and I have shared together.

And now here we are,
One week after you met my family
One week from the possibility of forever
And I'm not nervous, I'm excited!

It's hard to deny the connection we've made
True chemistry, total compatability, permanent friendship
All very important pieces to this puzzle of life
And you and I fit well together

So let's continue to fall forward
Piecing together this journey with new memories
Open to what is to come for us in the future
And excited to spend our lives together forever!

April 27, 2013
Antigua
@ 3:15pm

41. Last Thoughts

Date: April 29, 2013
Time: 1:45 PM
Location: Antigua

"Last Thoughts"

I stepped out of that limo with an open mind, but skeptical.
Unsure of what this experience would bring.
Then we started to talk and our relationship blossomed beautifully,
And I came to the realization that you are the one for me.

We've traveled this world together by plane, by boat, and helicopter,
Hand in hand over many seas.
And while THIS journey may be coming to an end,
I only see it as the beginning of something permanent for you and me.

So if there is one thing you can take from all that I've said
And we've experienced together,
Well alright maybe three.
Know that I am waiting for you to be by my side,
1. And I will always kiss you,
2. Tell you I love you,
3. And be there for you any time, wherever we may be.

I Love you Desiree.

Synopsis

This was my last opportunity to let Des know how I really felt about her, about this journey and about our future. I just got finished meeting her parents and needed to write her something. I was not able to share it with her at the time, but I ultimately shared it with her in person and truly meant every word. I wanted her to know that I wasn't going to stop loving her after this show or process or journey was over. I wanted her to know that my feelings were eternal and permanent and I only wanted to share my experiences in life with her and love her and grow old with her.

"Last Tango"

I stepped out of that [illegible] with [illegible], but skeptic
unsure of what this experience would bring
Then we started to talk and our relationship blossomed beautifully
And I came to the realization that you are the one for me.

We've traveled this world together by plane, boat, [illegible]
hand in hand across many seas
And while this journey may be coming to an end
I only see it as the beginning of something permanent for you + me.

So if there is one thing you can take from all that we've
said and we've experienced together.....
Well actually another three.
Know that I'm waiting for you to be by my side
And I will always miss you
Also that I love you
And be there for you any time, wherever we may be.

24 April 2013
[illegible]
@ 1:45 pm

42. Love and Support

Date: June 6, 2013
Time: 8:30 PM
Location: Airplane to Los Angeles

"Love and Support"

When I look at you I see forever,
A life I know I want to spend together.
The feelings I feel,
I know they are real,
You're the one and there is nobody better.

We have to make sure we stay strong,
For some days may be short and others seem long.
But you next to me,
This started on T.V.,
A bond unbreakable all along.

So please lean on me for support,
A rock I will be no matter how challenging the course.
I am here for you,
And behind all that you do,
I love you and I am FOREVER yours!

Synopsis

This is a preview into our new life together! I now get to look at Desiree for the rest of my life and nothing can replace the feelings I have for her. She means the world to me and without her I am nothing. I want nothing but to share everything with her. Coffee, family, friends, camping, trips, kids, our first house…everything.

Stanza four speaks to the trials and tribulations, joys and excitement that relationships inevitably have, and the importance of how we must stay the course and work through everything together to keep the bond we share "unbreakable." I wanted her to know and let her know everyday that she can "lean on me for support" and that I am there for her "no matter how challenging the course" may be in life. I tell her every day that I love her and I will tell her every day I love her for the rest of my life!

"Love and Support"

When I look at you I see forever,
A life I know I want to spend together.
The feelings I feel,
I know they are real,
You're the one and there is nobody better.

We have to make sure we stay strong
For some days may be short, and others seem long
But you next to me,
This [illegible] by us,
A bond unbreakable all along.

So always lean on me for support
A rock I will be no matter how challenging the course.
I am here for you,
And behind all that you do
I love you and I am forever yours!

June 6th, 2013
Airplane to LA
@ 8:30pm

Poems by Des

43. Charming and Handsome

Date: April 5, 2013
Time: 2:45 PM
Location: Plane from Germany to Spain

"Charming and Handsome"

From the first night, one knee on the ground
Charming and handsome, instant attraction was found.

At the dodge ball game, it was apparent-no shame.
On top of that roof, overlooking that view,
That was the moment, I knew sparks grew.

As our hearts are open, thoughts expressed,
Memories of lederhosen create a beautiful picture-
I must confess.

Still the twinkle in your eye, reflects your heart that's
alive.
Never ponder why, trusting your every line,
Keeping in mind love can come at anytime.

The strength that you show, is the patience I know.
At times can be hard to withstand,
But I'm here holding your hand.

As the clock ticks, timing never late,
For the connections to form from each and every date
And the rose to one day grant us our fate.

I look forward to the unknown
Appreciate the emotion you have shown,
And hopeful to see if in your heart,
I have found a home.

Synopsis

This is a poem I wrote for Chris after our time we spent together in Germany. Relationships were developing and I knew Chris and I had something special so I wanted to share my feelings with him in writing. There are many hidden metaphors here so I hope you can find them and enjoy reading it as much as I enjoyed writing it!

- ***Des***

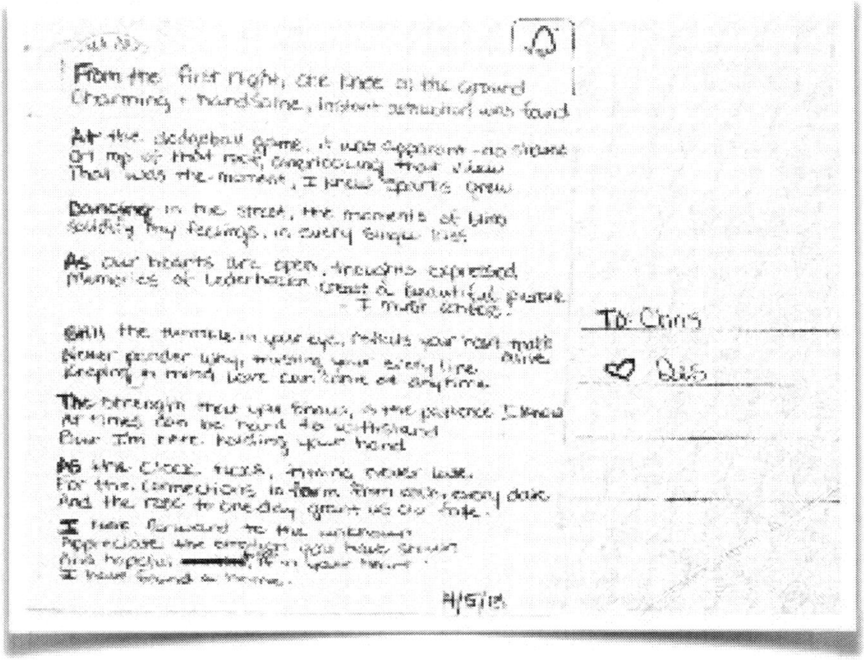

From the first night, one knee on the ground
Charming + handsome, instant attraction was found

At the dodgeball game, it was apparent [illegible]
On top of that [illegible], [illegible] that view
That was the moment, I knew sparks grew

Dancing in the street, the moments of [illegible]
solidify my feelings, in every single kiss.

As our hearts are open, thoughts expressed,
Memories of [illegible] create a beautiful picture
- I must confess!

With the twinkle in your eye, [illegible] your heart melt
Never ponder why, trusting your every line. alive
Keeping in mind love can come at anytime.

The strength that you shows, & the patience I know
At times can be hard to withstand
But I'm here, holding your hand

As the clock ticks, time never [illegible].
For the connections in form from each, every date
And the road to one day grant us our fate.

I look forward to the unknown
Appreciate the emotion you have shown
And hopeful [illegible] it in your heart
I have found a home.

4/5/18

To: Chris

♡ [illegible]

44. Honest and True

Date: May 4, 2013
Time: 4:25 PM
Location: Antigua

"Honest and True"

On my face, I wear a grin from ear to ear,
Knowing my heart and mind have come so far.
Hand in hand, I finally see clear
Realizing the choices that have kept you here.

The journey we've been on, short yet long
Remind me of the feelings you have shown
In all the moments our love has grown.
I know now, my heart is where you belong.

The joy you bring in every kiss
Are the sparks my body feels
And not only the characteristics checked off the list,
But the moments that ensure eternal bliss.

The weeks behind us, is the time that's passed
What lies before us, is the true test
To see if this will last.

My life wants, what the heart feels
A loyal man by my side, honest and true
Knowing the love I can give, all of my days

I want only to invest and give it all to you!

Love Always,

Desiree

Synopsis

This is a piece I wrote for Chris when I knew he was The One. I wanted to express to him how I felt and that I loved him in the same poetic form he would communicate to me. The poem wasn't given to him until after his beautiful proposal but will be a poem he will have forever along with my love.

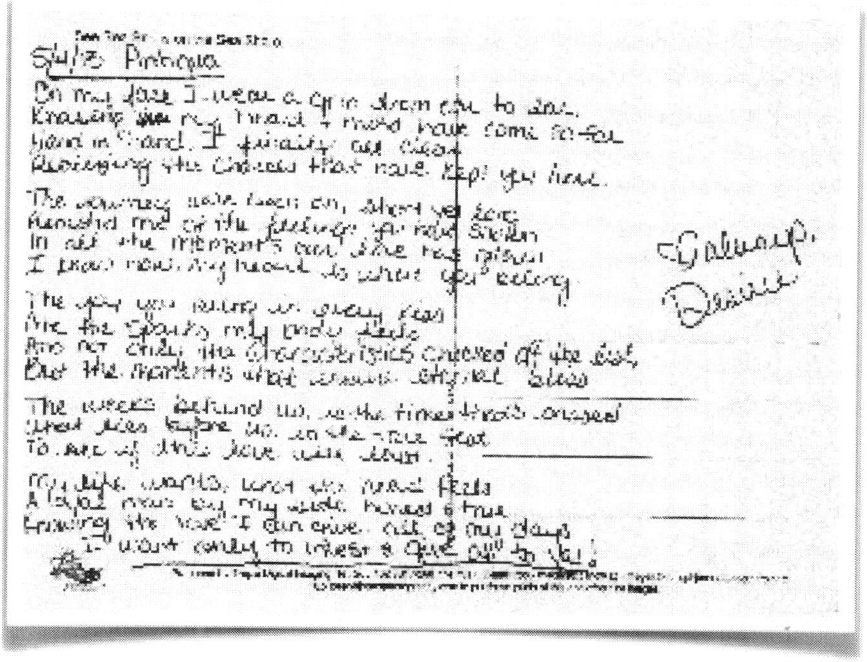

5/4/13 Antigua

On my face I wear a grin drawn ear to ear.
Knowing my heart + mind have come so far
hand in hand. I finally see clear
Realizing the choices that have kept you here.

The journey we've been on, short yet long
Reminded me of the feelings you have shown
In all the moments and time has given
I know now, my heart is where you belong!

The joy you bring in every way
Are the sparks my body feels
And not only the characteristics checked off the list,
But the moments that remain [illegible] [illegible]

The weeks behind us, as the times that's [illegible]
What lies before us, in the [illegible] that
To [illegible] of this love will [illegible].

My life wants, what the heart feels
A loyal man by my side, honest + true
Knowing the love I can give, all of my days
I want only to invest + give all to you!

Always,
Desiree

New Poetry

45. Memories Remembered

Date: August 24, 2009
Time: 1:24 AM
Location: Daytona Beach, FL
By: Chris

"Memories Remembered"

Sometimes when you sit and think,
Of all the people you've met in life.
Outside of family there are only a few,
You can call and those feelings hold true.

Feelings of true care and friendship,
The memories of past they stick so strong,
Forever printed in the mind as days go by,
Recalled upon when days seem too long.

Memories that help the mind when troubled,
For the feelings tied to them are such:
Compassion, honesty and loyalty.
Never are those feelings ever so loved.

When one may be out and on their own,
Away from the daily routine of life
And all the people who were close,
Those memories are ones they look to cling.

Synopsis

I wrote this poem as I sat on the deck of my condo in Daytona Beach one evening. Being away from family and friends for long periods of time allows one to sit and reminisce on the past and realize how much one values good, quality relationships. I was building new relationships daily with friends on the ball field, but I would always visit those memories of friends back home who knew me as something more than just a baseball player.

"Memories Remembered"

Sometimes when you sit and think,
Of all the people you've met in life,
Outside of family there are only a few,
You can call and those feelings hold true

Feelings of true care and friendship,
The memories of past they stick so strong,
Forever printed in the mind as days go by,
Recalled when days seem too long.

Memories that help the mind when troubled,
For the feelings tied to them are such,
Of compassion, honesty, and loyalty,
Never are those feelings ever so loved.

When one may be out and on their own,
Away from the daily routine
Of life and all the people who were close,
Those memories are ones they hold to cling.

24 August 2004 1:15a
Daytona Beach, Florida

46. Sunrise

Date: May 29, 2009
Time: 5:25 AM
Location: Bus Ride To Michigan
By: Chris

"Sunrise"

How many times we sit and wonder,
Oh so early in the day.
What time will it rise this morning,
On this early last day in May.

The morning sun will rise,
With colors the sky won't deprive.
From red to blue, orange, yellow and gray,
Won't the sun rise every day?

For times you think its hidden behind,
The clouds she brings fog the mind.
But sun is there for no life without,
Rise and fall there is no doubt.

The rays the keep us warm,
Farmers crops do adore.
Bring life to all the plants we eat,
The sun created, God's great feat.

Until it is over head,
Chance there is, we're still in bed.

For our day ends when rest world sleeps,
Night crawlers we're not but dreams we keep.

Synopsis

As you read this allow your mind to wonder. It was something I wrote very early in the morning on a bus ride in Michigan. Sometimes it was hard to sleep on the bus rides from city to city. I would find myself awake watching the sun rise and pondering life and all of its beauty.

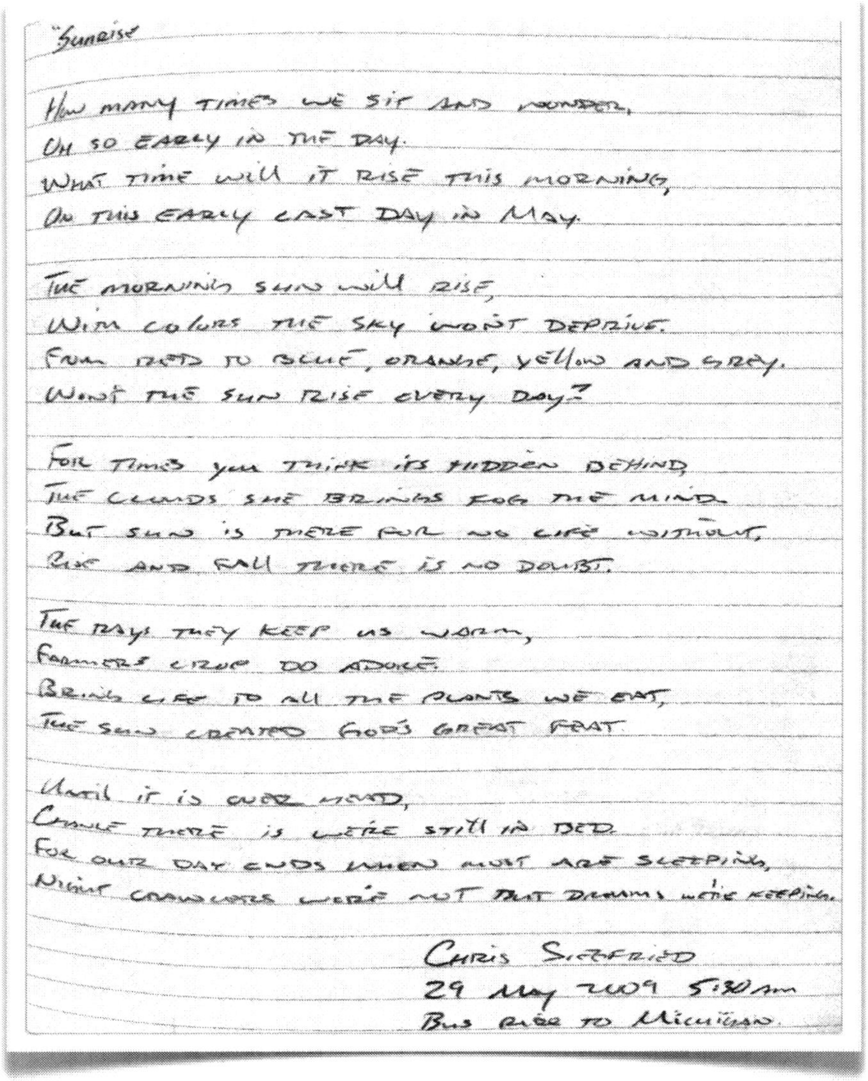

"Sunrise"

How many times we sit and wonder,
Oh so early in the day.
What time will it rise this morning,
On this early last day in May.

The morning sun will rise,
With colors the sky won't deprive.
From red to blue, orange, yellow and grey.
Won't the sun rise every day?

For times you think its hidden behind,
The clouds she brings fog the mind.
But sun is there for no life without,
Rise and fall there is no doubt.

The rays they keep us warm,
Farmers crop do adore.
Bring life to all the plants we eat,
The sun created God's great feat.

Until it is over head,
Chance there is we're still in bed.
For our day ends when most are sleeping,
Night crawlers we're not but dreams we're keeping.

Chris Siegfried
29 May 2009 5:30 am
Bus ride to Michigan.

47. The Voice Unheard

Date: April 22, 2009
Time: 4:00 PM
Location: Starbucks
By: Chris

"The Voice Unheard"

Each day anew brings something different,
She's not quite sure what to expect.
Her surroundings are so ever changing,
But she pushes through with no regrets.

It's the smaller things in life that bring her joy,
The hearts and souls untouched, both girls and boys.
With family, friends and music near,
Life's in perspective, but paths not so clear…sometimes.

She turns to song for consoling pleasure,
Some of her favorites to hard to measure.
Yet songs she sings full of life and cheer,
For both crowds of young and last days to near.

When that day does come,
Degree in hand,
She may ask to sing,
But please not band.

For her voice and goals,
Both strong and sincere.

She'll touch all hearts,
Protect your ears.

Synopsis

This piece is about my sister Ahna and her love she has for the kids she teaches and the music she sings. Ahna has been a singer since she was a child and went to college to study both music and elementary education. My family, along with others, had the opportunity to watch Ahna sing for school functions as well as local jazz clubs. I am proud of her and thankful she is in my life.

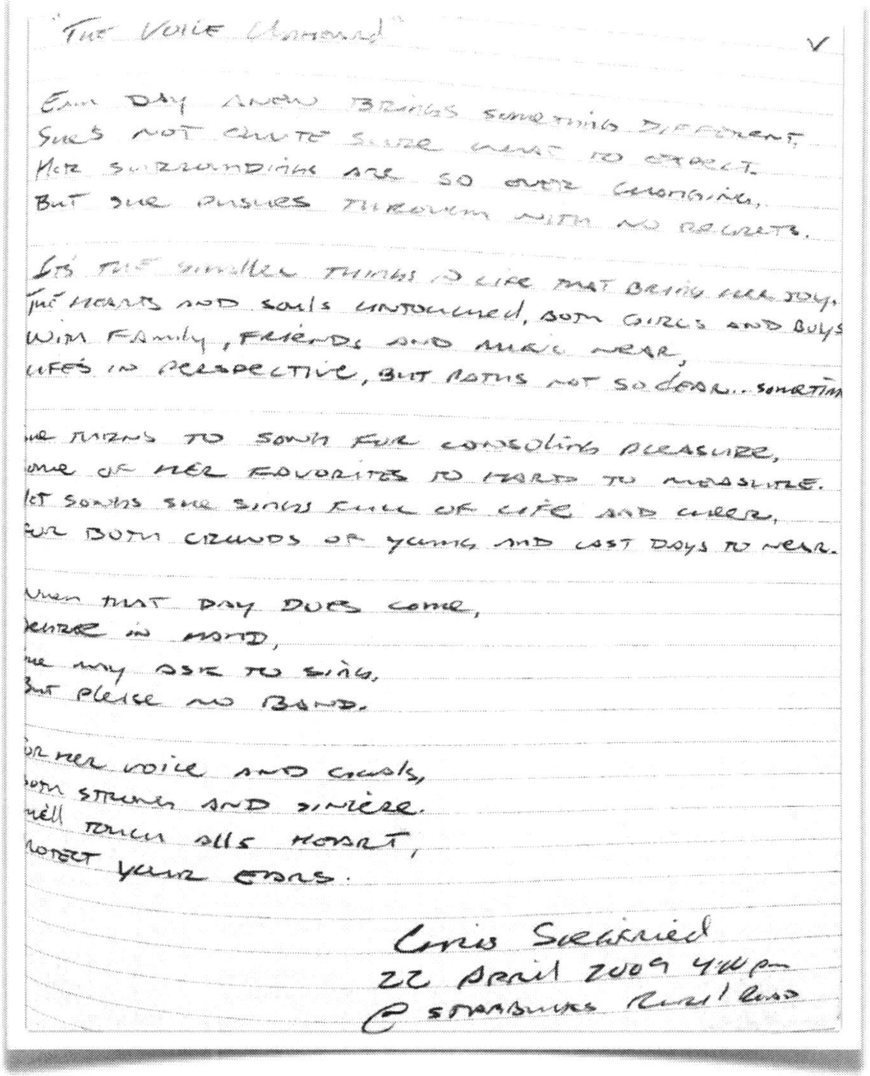

"The Voice Diamond"

√

Each day anew brings something different,
She's not quite sure what to expect.
Her surroundings are so ever changing,
But she pushes through with no regrets.

It's the smaller things in life that bring her joy.
The hearts and souls untouched, both girls and boys
With family, friends and music near,
Life's in perspective, but paths not so clear... sometim

he turns to song for consoling pleasure,
one of her favorites to hard to measure.
ct songs she sings full of life and cheer,
or both crowds of young and last days to near.

hen that day does come,
ure in mind,
he may ask to sing,
ut please no band.

or her voice and vocals,
oth strong and sincere.
he'll touch all's heart,
rotect your ears.

Chris Siegfried
22 April 2009 4:40 pm
@ Starbucks Russell Road

48. Worry Less

Date: May 19, 2009
Time: 1:45 PM
Location: Beloit, WI
By: Chris

"Worry Less"

Why does one worry so much?
For life you may lose touch.
The goals you set,
The plans not met,
No feel for everything, a rush.

What if you were to step back,
For goals and plans then attacked.
The mind at ease,
For then you'd please,
Feel everything relaxed.

So when you mind does wonder,
Don't worry when you ponder.
Let your mind be free,
For then you'll see,
You'll feel stronger ever longer.

Synopsis

This poem was written for those who have a harder time focusing on the bigger picture rather than what is going on in "the now". Remember to always keep things in perspective and realize that what you do now can and will have an outcome in your future. Do not worry about doing things perfectly all of the time. Sometimes doing the best you can is all you can request of yourself. It is important to have goals and reach for the stars; It gives you balance and confidence.

"Worry Less"

Why does one worry so much?
For life you may lose touch
The goals you set
The plans not met
No feel for everything a rush.

What if you were to step back,
For goals and plans then attacked
The mind at ease,
For then you'd please,
Feel everything relaxed.

So when your mind does wander,
Don't worry when you ponder.
Let your mind be free,
For then you'll see,
You'll feel stronger ever longer

-Chris Siegfried
19 May 2009 1:45pm
Beloit Wisconsin Starbucks

49. Subconscious Mind

Date: July 15, 2009
Time: 12:00 PM
Location: Grand Rapids, MI
By: Chris

"Subconscious Mind"

The mind does play tricks some do wonder,
Where the subconscious mind may roam.
If its not this or that, it must be the other,
Kept deep inside the mind unknown.

Sometimes there are feelings all tangled inside,
Only to surface when something may trigger.
It may be a song or verse read in scripture.
Unlocking the magic that lies in the mind.

It chooses its path in more ways then one,
Throughout your life there are signs.
Do not ignore all of these messages,
That lie so deep within the mind.

With feelings of those thoughts within,
Emotions may begin to stir.
Control your thoughts and emotions dampened,
Like was on a well lit fire.

Subconscious mind so deep inside,

The memories so well kept and hidden!
Continue to grow and experiences will bring,
New memories for you to listen.

Synopsis

This is an interesting poem that I wrote while riding a bus for about five hours to the next city we were going to play in.

Sometimes while I write I let my mind be the guide to my pen. Stanza one opens the reader up to the idea that if you do sit there and just be still, your mind will start to wander and unique thoughts will start to formulate in your mind.

Have you ever been driving along and a song comes on the radio that brings you back to a moment in life that you loved, a girl or guy you dated, a place you visited or a person you met? At that moment, experiences - whether good or bad - start coming back to you. Experiences and feelings locked deep inside your mind that may never have come up if it weren't for that "trigger" that unlocked them.

I recommend you try this exercise. Try and sit in quiet or somewhere in nature where all you hear is the air around you and let your mind wander. Bring a notepad and write down whatever it is that comes to mind.

"Subconscious Mind" ✓

The mind does play tricks some to wonder,
Where the subconscious mind may roam.
If its not this or that, it must be the other,
Kept deep inside the mind unknown.

Sometimes there are feelings all tangled inside,
Only to surface when something may trigger.
It may be a song or verse read in scripture,
Unlocking the magic that lies in the mind.

It chooses its path in more ways than one,
Throughout your life there are signs.
Do not ignore all of these messages,
That lie so deep within the mind.

With feelings of these thoughts within,
Emotions may begin to stir.
Control your minds and emotions dampened,
Like water on a well lit fire.

Subconscious mind so deep inside,
The memories so well kept and hidden!
Continue to grow and experiences will bring
New memories for you to listen.

15 July 2009 12:00p
Busride to Grand Rapids MI

50. Secret

Date: May 19, 2013
Time: 2:50 PM
Location: Los Angeles, CA
By: Desiree

"Secret"

A secret beyond our control
Kept in a locket under our hearts
Keeps our lips tight so others won't know
A love story has blossomed, our desire to show

The sunsets and passing stars
Are the hands of time
Till I can see you again
But know that my love will never be too far

The chatter upon our lips
Brought to life by satellites
Is the affection we long for in the night
But in the morning terribly miss

The distance far and wide
Can never remove the rope that binds us
It is for eternity, my love
And with that promise, I come alive

Such joy in the thoughts of you and I

The life to come, a family and home
Hopeful beginnings to share together
Lasting memories of a love never-ending

The day that you got down on one knee
Is the day I handed you my heart
The happiness within will never subside
For this secret is a piece in our story
That will soon play its part.

Synopsis

This poem means a lot to me because it was written during the time that Chris and I were away from each other and had to keep our relationship a secret. We wanted nothing more than to be with each other and the love I felt for him continued to grow each day while apart. We talked on the phone or Skyped about 3 times a day and although that seems like a lot, all we wanted was to be together and talk in person. Although keeping our relationship a secret was hard to do, it is still a part of our relationship that both of us will cherish and never forget.

5/19/13

Secret

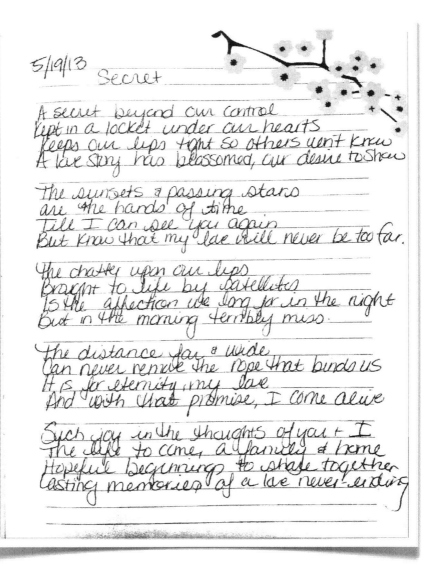

A secret beyond our control
Kept in a locket under our hearts
Keeps our lips tight so others won't know
A love story has blossomed, our desire to show

The sunsets & passing stars
are the hands of time
Till I can see you again
But know that my love will never be too far.

The chatter upon our lips
Brought to life by satellites
Is the affection we long for in the night
But in the morning terribly miss.

The distance far & wide
Can never remove the rope that binds us
It is for eternity, my love
And with that promise, I come alive

Such joy in the thoughts of you + I
The life to come, a family & home
Hopeful beginnings to share together
Lasting memories of a love never-ending

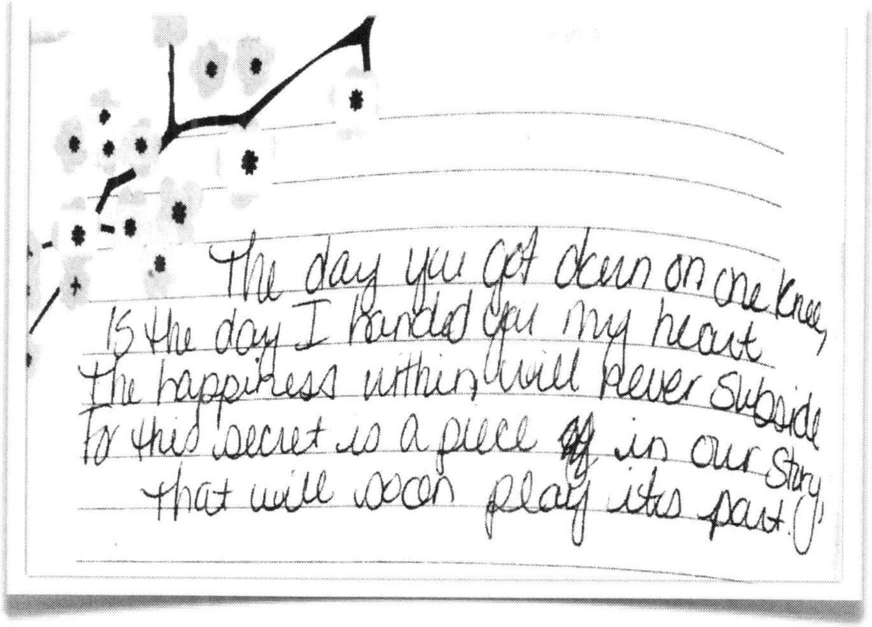
The day you got down on one knee,
Is the day I handed you my heart
The happiness within will never subside
For this secret is a piece of in our story
that will soon play its part.

51. Rose

Date: October 8, 2012
Time: 2:40 PM
Location: Los Angeles, CA
By: Desiree

"Rose"

Petals form a majestic peak
In its beauty, all hearts seek
Magnetic force, feelings reach
The hope it takes, no words could teach

Hanging on the verbal pause
Awaiting the damage it can cause
Formal lines stand unsteady
On their towers, weak but ready

The scarlet prize, shines its light
Embraces the ones, chosen at night

Synopsis

I actually wrote this poem while filming, about a rose ceremony. It is about all of the girls that were lined up in their stilettos, waiting to hear their names called aloud to make it through to another day. It is about how everyone sees the rose as a trophy to continue on.

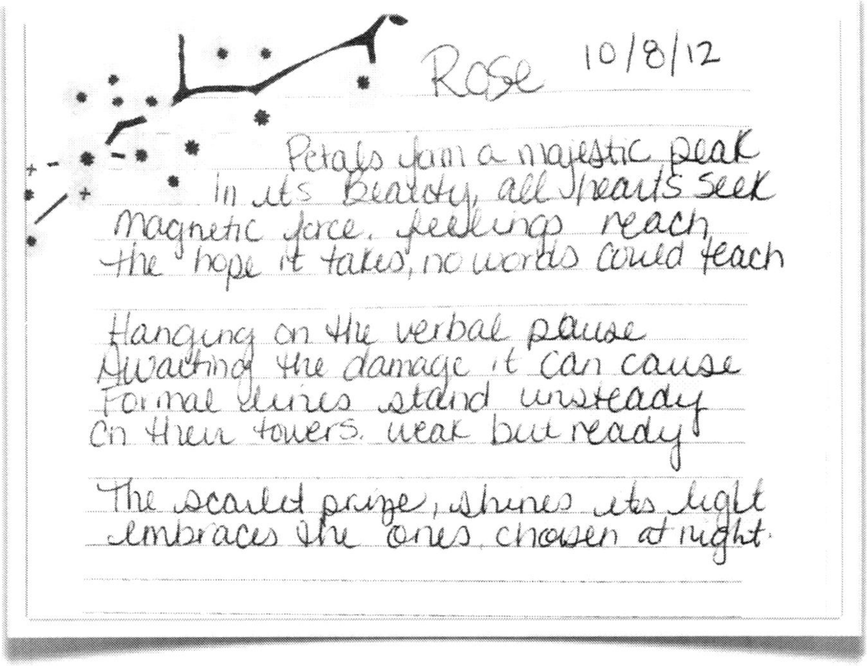

Rose 10/8/12

Petals form a majestic peak
In its Beauty, all hearts seek
Magnetic force, feelings reach
the hope it takes, no words could teach

Hanging on the verbal pause
Awaiting the damage it can cause
Formal lines stand unsteady
On their towers, weak but ready

The scarlet prize, shines its light
embraces the ones chosen at night.

52. Beauty

Date: June 9, 2011
Time: 5:15 PM
Location: Antigua
By: Desiree

"Beauty"

The scent of roses all around
Vibrant colors blind
A flourishing garden
This is beauty in my eyes

The giggling laugh of a child
A joyous noise to hear
Such beauty as the waves flow
Perfectly in line

The silent touch of the brushing wind
As the warmth of the blazing sun shines

Beauty seldom recognized.

The trust in a friend's eye
An honest hug binds
Family to turn to, in the deepest times

What beauty in a life.

A gentle kiss from a lover's lips

Embraces the heart and love is felt

Beauty in a guiding hand
To help and hold
When times are tight

A sincere smile
From a stranger
Whom you will never meet

Images brought to life
From an artist, living on the street

Change in his pocket
Given to a child
For a chance to eat

This life we live, is ours to take
And make it what we like

The beauty in our lives
Is what we make it to be
Through our eyes.

Synopsis

There is beauty everywhere we look yet so much of that beauty is taken for granted and not seen at all. When I sat down to write this poem I thought about all of the things I see as beautiful. Not just visually beautiful but what true beauty really means to me. The actions we take or the relationships we make are so beautiful if we can look at them in a different way. I wanted this poem to be a challenge to take each day as a gift and realize that what I see as beautiful is dependent on how I see my life and those around me.

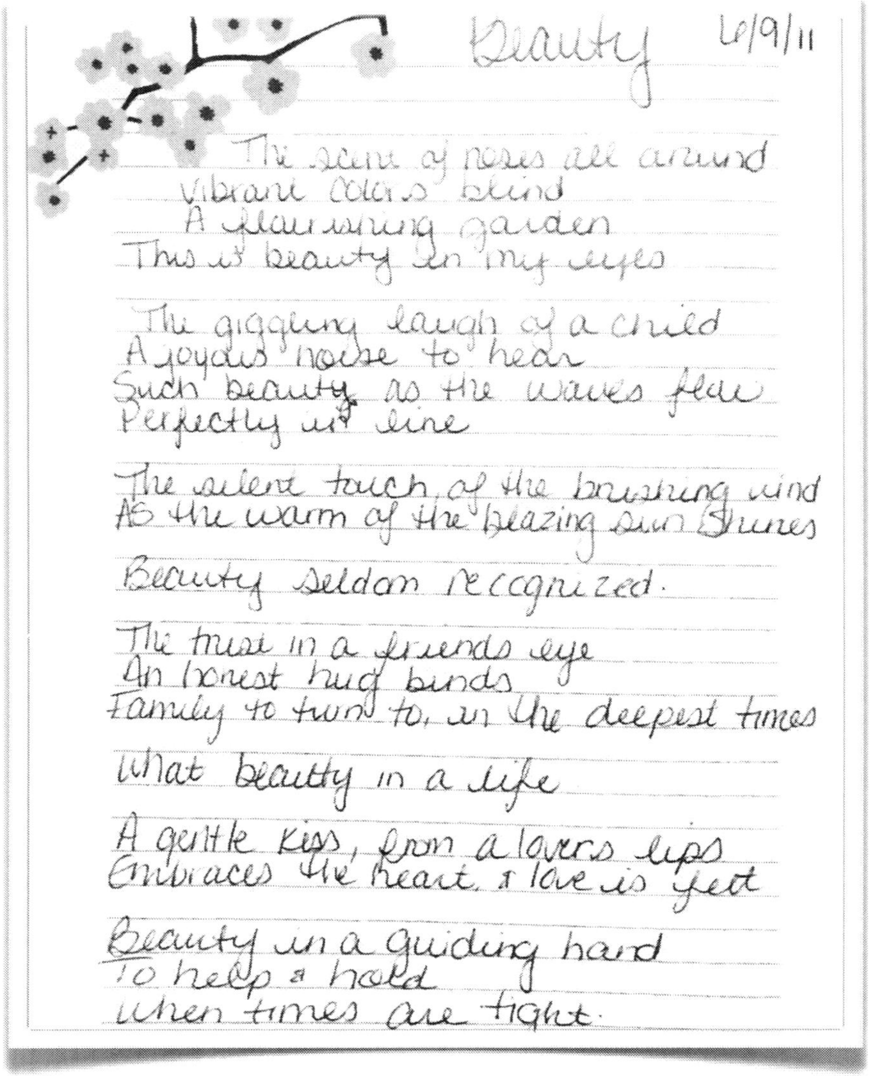

Beauty 6/9/11

The scent of roses all around
Vibrant colors blind
A flourishing garden
This is beauty in my eyes

The giggling laugh of a child
A joyous noise to hear
Such beauty as the waves flow
Perfectly in line

The silent touch of the brushing wind
AS the warm of the blazing sun shines
Beauty seldom recognized.

The trust in a friends eye
An honest hug binds
Family to turn to, in the deepest times
What beauty in a life

A gentle kiss, from a lovers lips
Embraces the heart & love is felt

Beauty in a guiding hand
To help & hold
when times are tight.

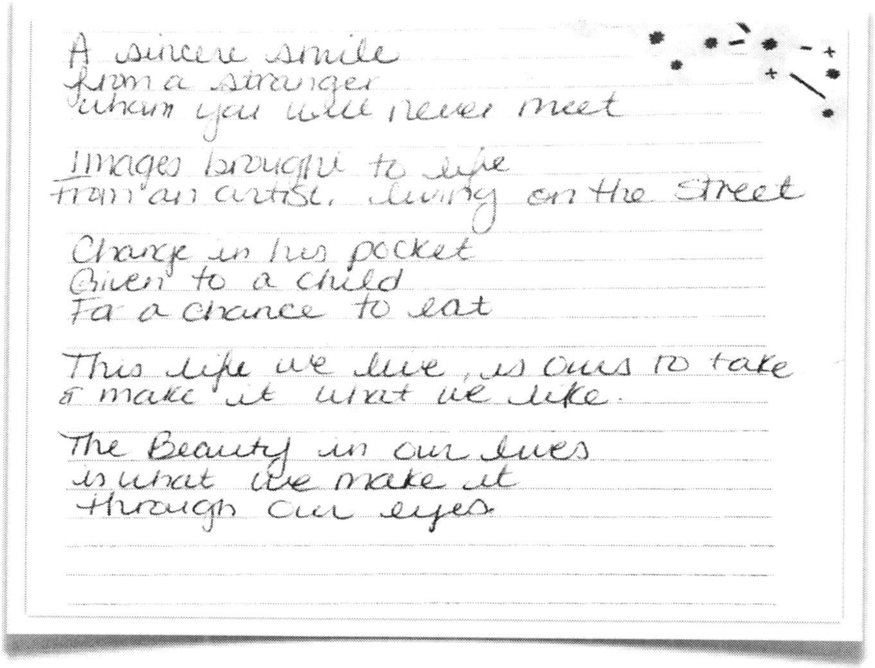

A sincere smile
from a stranger
whom you will never meet

Images brought to life
from an artist, living on the street

Change in his pocket
Given to a child
For a chance to eat

This life we live, is ours to take
& make it what we like.

The Beauty in our lives
is what we make it
through our eyes.

53. Colors of the Heart

Date: June 17, 2011
Time: 10:38 PM
Location: Los Angeles, CA
By: Desiree

"Colors of the Heart"

This heart of mine is bleeding out
Colors of hope, shades that shine

At times the colors blind
Filled with joy they cannot be confined

With the daily grind
The palette of colors combine
Mixing hues into shades undefined

RED with confusion, the heart bleeds more
Choices to be made to open that door

Colors pour out, the rain washes through
Blank canvas is left, to start another day new

Waves of BLUE, run their course
Occasionally calm
But most with crashing force

The gloom is lifted, skies become warm
What the heart feels
Is YELLOW hues charm

Relax on the hills of GREEN
Find comfort and shade
Under the flourishing tree

Calm of the RAINBOW
Brushes where you lay
Heart set free
Peace to guide your way

Hope, love, peace
Regret, confusion tease

The crayon you choose, will make its mark
Color bleeds, fills the heart.

Synopsis

Each day we choose the mood we want to be in and our daily struggles can affect those moods throughout the day. This poem is a fun way to see our life in color and shares different colors for the moods that change throughout our day. Sometimes stress can be too much and all we see is red, but luckily we always start a new day that leaves a blank canvas for us to choose what to do with. It's our outlook that affects the colors we see and this poem was a reminder for me to choose what I wanted my day to be.

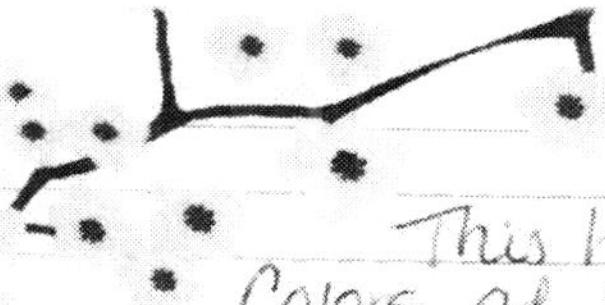

Colors of the Heart

6/17/11

This heart of mine, is bleeding out
Colors of hope, shades that shine

At times, the colors blend
filled with joy, they cannot be confined

With the daily grind
The palette of colors combine
mixing hues into shades undefined

Red with confusion, the heart bleeds more
Choices to be made, to open that door

Colors pour out, the rain washes through
Blank canvas is left, to start another day new

Waves of Blue run their course
Occasionally calm
But most with crashing force

The gloom is lifted, skies become warm
What the heart feels
is yellow hues charm

Relax on the hills of Green.
Find comfort & shade
under the flourishing tree

→

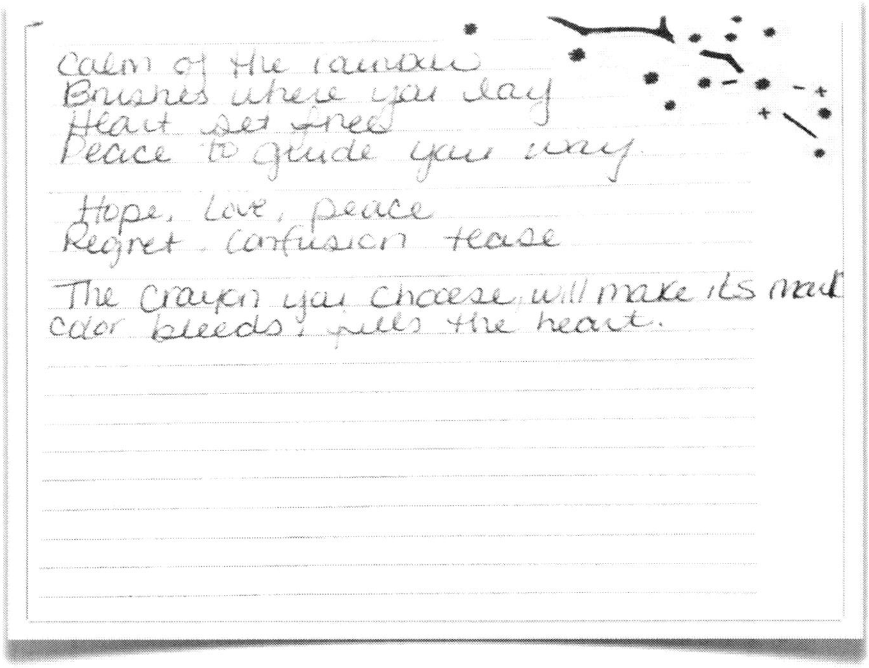

Calm of the rainbow
Brushes where you lay
Heart set free
Peace to guide your way.

Hope, Love, peace
Regret. Confusion tease

The crayon you choose, will make its mark
color bleeds, fills the heart.

54. Step Out

Date: June 30, 2010
Time: 7:15 PM
Location: Los Angeles, CA
By: Desiree

"Step Out"

You are who you want to be
So open that door
Feel the breeze

Step out
Don't be afraid
For I am with you
And will never leave

Don't contemplate
Just motivate
And you will see
You are who you want to be

The journey's long
Keep the road steady
Can't go anywhere
Without the pedal heavy

Dig down deep

There you will find
What's been hiding
All this time

The magnitude
What you can do
The passion
You feel and see

Can never be taken
Away from you
For you are who you want to be.

Synopsis

There were many people and friends around me during this time that were confused and clueless on what they wanted to do with their lives. Whether it was making a decision to leave an unhappy job place for something more or to step out and realize what they needed. I felt lucky that I had a passion to design and wanted my friends to realize what their passions were. This poem came about due to the struggle they had with what they wanted to do.

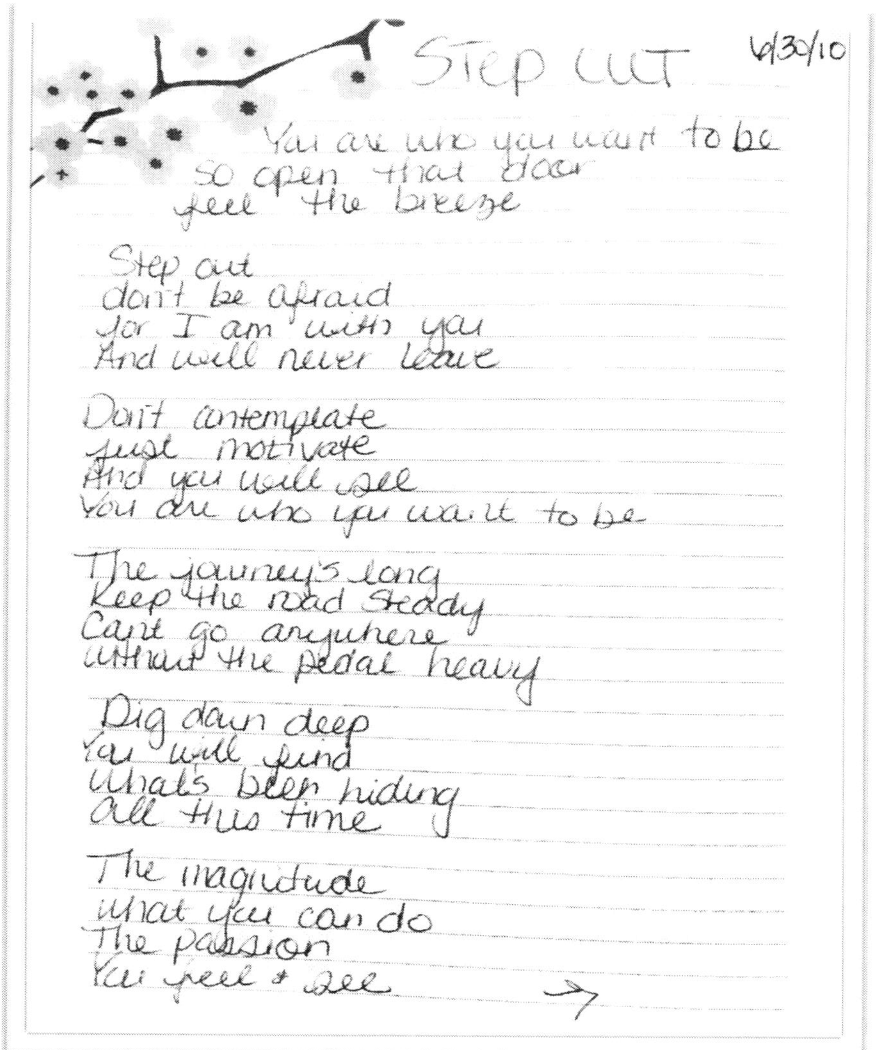

Step Out 6/30/10

You are who you want to be
so open that door
feel the breeze

Step out
don't be afraid
for I am with you
And will never leave

Don't contemplate
just motivate
And you will see
You are who you want to be

The journey's long
Keep the road steady
Can't go anywhere
without the pedal heavy

Dig down deep
You will find
What's been hiding
all this time

The magnitude
what you can do
The passion
You feel + see

→

→

Can never be taken
away from you
For you are who you want to be!

55. Butterfly

Date: October 10, 2011
Time: 3:45 PM
Location: Los Angeles, CA
By: Desiree

"Butterfly"

Like a butterfly
Journey not always Grande

Not until the day she sees Your light
You take her by the hand

Colors shine of beauty
Once confined and hidden from the world

You breathe Joy
Grace, a wind to forever swirl

The wings given
To fulfill the path and script
Of His will

She soars on high
Freedom in every stroke
To a place of Faith
Enduring with hope

Forever guided she will be

The wonder she creates
Is His glory upon her
For all to see

Oh the places she can go
All the people she can meet
The flowers of wonder
His world she will seek

With clouds around her
She flies strong
To a place of safety
A place to call home

His light will forever
Spotlight the beauty He illuminates

A symbol of His creation
From the colors to the core

His love, a mighty breath
To help her forever soar.

Synopsis

The butterfly is a beautiful creature that doesn't start out that way. Like a butterfly I felt my life changing in an unexplainable way. I was becoming more confident and secure in myself while my heart was growing in my faith. The outlook I had on my life became even more positive than I could have ever thought it to be. I was going through a struggle at this time but I knew that my trust in the Lord would forever see me through and this poem reflects the hope that I felt. While I wrote this I also imagined all of my girlfriends as this butterfly that will not focus on her struggle but let her true beauty and confidence allow her to go far in this life.

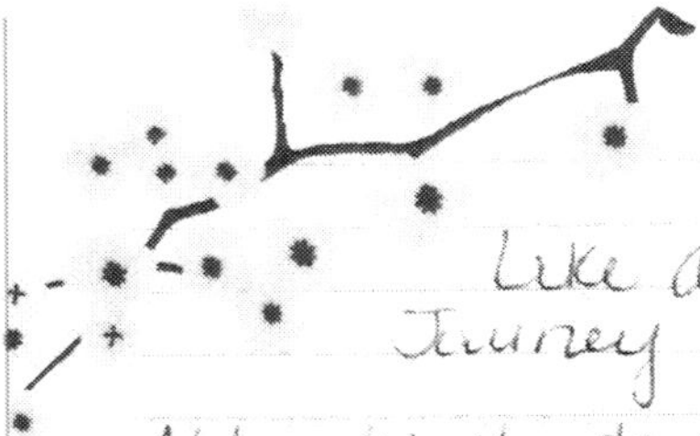

10/22/11

Butterfly

Like a butterfly
Journey not always Grande

Not until the day, she sees Your Light
You take her by the hand

Colors shine of Beauty
Once confined, & hidden from the world

You breathe Joy
Grace, a wind to forever swirl

The wings given
To fulfill the path & script
of His will

She soars on high
Freedom in every stroke
To a place of Faith
enduring w/ hope.

Forever guided she will be
The wonder she creates
is His Glory upon her
for all to see

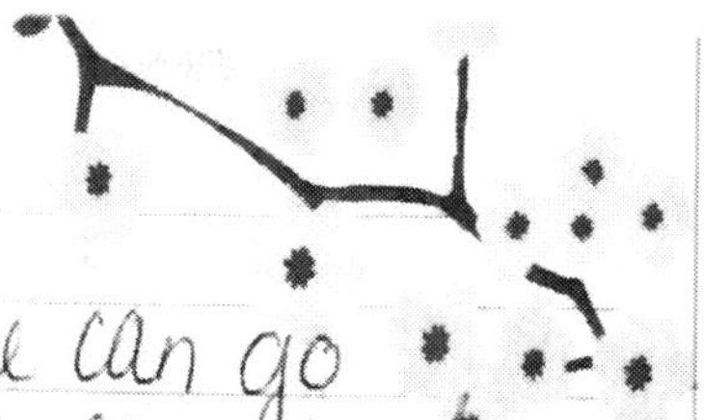

Oh the places she can go
All the people she can meet
The flowers of wonder
His world she will seek.

With clouds around her
She flies strong
To a place of safety
a place to call home

His light will forever
spotlight the beauty He illuminates

A symbol of His creation
From the rocks to the core

His love, a mighty breath
To help her forever soar.

The Proposal

From Desiree:

Never in a million years did I imagine to meet a man with such confidence and love in his heart. From the moment Chris and I had our first conversation there was a calmness and comfort I had never felt with anyone else I had dated before. He was quirky yet charming and his ability to be himself made me love him more and more each time we saw each other. Chris was never shy about how he felt towards me and that was something I was never used to in past relationships so it was something to get used to but also what set him apart and made him so very special to me.

Each time Chris and I would hang out he would surprise me with something new, and the fact that we shared an interest in poetry made us even closer.
The fact that Chris and I could feel comfortable being ourselves right away, have great conversation (funny and serious), play sports together, and always stay in the moment made it feel like I had known him forever, like we were high school sweethearts. Chris is everything I could ever wish for as the father of my children, husband and best friend. That is why there was no doubt in my mind that I wanted to spend the rest of my life with him when he got down on one knee to propose.
There was so much I wanted to say to Chris before he proposed to me and unlike most proposals I had the opportunity to prepare for anything. I wanted to tell him

how much I loved him and that I wanted to grow old together! Through thick and thin. ;)

As Chris walked up to me, I couldn't help but have a smile from ear to ear. He looked SO handsome and nervous that I wanted to run right up to him and kiss him! He looked so nervous that for a second I got worried but once he started talking I felt at ease and in that moment like we were the only two people in the world. In the middle of talking Chris grabbed my face and laid a heavy kiss on me that I will never forget. When he got down on his knee, I was so enwrapped in the moment I almost forgot to even look at the ring.

His proposal was the happiest day of my life and a moment I will cherish for eternity. I will always remember his leg shaking, eyes twinkling, and words said that changed our lives forever. I am so lucky to have Chris in my life and am grateful for everyday that I get to spend with him. I can't wait to marry him and begin another chapter of our lives together.

From Chris:

There was no doubt in my mind that I wanted to be with Desiree for the rest of my life. She was and is the best woman I have ever met inside and out, and I knew that if she were to say "yes," we were going to continue something great together.

The night before I proposed to Des might have been the most nerve-racking night of my life. I was confident in what Des and I shared together, all of our experiences and our journey to get to know each other, but there was the slight possibility that she may not have been as ready as I was at the time. I stayed up all night trying to figure out what I wanted to tell her; I already knew what I wanted to ask her. To me it was more than just asking her if she would marry me. I truly wanted her to know that I was committed to her and to sharing my life with her, growing old together, having a family and raising children together, building and working on a long lasting relationship until we were 104 years old! She was and is the one for me and I knew it.

After getting about five hours of sleep I woke up the next morning to take a walk on the beach as the sun was rising. I needed to be by myself and just think about everything that was going on and what was about to happen. As I sat there in the sand and looked out over the Caribbean, an excitement came over me! I was fully ready to embark on a new life together with Desiree. When I walked up to her, all I could think at that moment was how beautiful she looked and how lucky I would be if she were to say yes.

As I stood in front of her and recalled all the moments we shared together, I couldn't help but notice how nervous I was and how my legs would not stop shaking! She looked so amazing and she was so poised. She too wanted to say a few words and while it caught me off guard at first, I could see that look in her eye that told me she wanted to be with me for the rest of our lives.
As I got down on one knee I wanted to make sure I said her entire name…and not drop the ring as I pulled it out of my pocket. Then the words came out, "Desiree Eileen Hartsock- will you marry me?" She said yes, my heart

stopped beating 200 miles per hour and I gave her the most memorable kiss and hug I will ever share with her, well maybe the second most memorable once we get married. I was and am the happiest guy in the world and am so lucky Des and I found each other, even if it was on TV!

Life after the Proposal from Des:

Seattle is such a wonderful place to live and after being long distance for about 3 months I decided to move here from California to be with Chris. If we wanted our relationship to work we knew that we would have to start it together in the same place and start fresh. Chris' poetry has always been important to him since it was an outlet during his years playing baseball. To put his poems together in a memoir was an accomplishment of his that he always wanted to do and I'm so proud of all of his work.

We look forward to planning our wedding and also sharing that experience with everyone. Being engaged is such a wonderful time as a couple and both of us are enjoying the moments leading up to that big day!

Photos

Chris and his Dad.

Pitching in Spring Training.

Playing for the Cubs' High A team in Florida.

Pitching for the Pilots.

Des and Chris in LA.

Great shot by Des in Antigua.

Lazy day together.

We love having fun :)

LA life before moving to Seattle.

Des and Chris at their engagement party.

Right after the world knew.

Road trip to our new home in Seattle.

Fun dinner in Santa Monica.

One of our favorite spots to hike.

Love her.

Kisses.

Silly kids.

Got invited to the Seahawks game by Pete Carroll!

At Junior League Seattle for a book signing with a fan.

Meeting Pete Carroll and going onto the field for a Seahawks game was an honor.

Date night in Seattle, cuddling to stay warm!

On the dance floor at Chris' sister, Ahna's wedding. All the right dance moves come out with sunglasses on!

Desiree on the ferris wheel documenting Chris' fear of heights.

Bridal event and runway show that we attended to support our friend Luly Yang.

Gala event with some friends to support the Northwest Kidney Center.

Hanging with Jason and Molly Mesnik. They're so great!

Chris playing around with pumpkins at a pumpkin patch in Oregon.

Cheesin' for the camera. Peace!

Chris on the ferris wheel freaking out because he is afraid of heights.

Back to where Chris' hometown date took place for his sister's wedding.

Desiree found her pumpkin!

Desiree and Chris at Dinner with Friends on top of the world!

Desiree and Chris catching up on some Blues Music at a local blues hall.

Happy hour with each other on Lake Union!

Ahna (Chris' sister) and Jeff's Wedding!

Chris and Des finding their first pumpkin.

Chris and Des celebrating their relationship with friends.

Chris and Des out on the town with friends!

LOVE.

Thank You!

Thank you so much for reading through Diamonds + Hearts. We can't wait to continue to share our new life with you! Don't forget to sign up for our email list at DHpoetry.com!

30424600R00139

Made in the USA
Lexington, KY
02 March 2014